T0155516

SpringerBriefs in Computer Science

SpringerBriefs present concise summaries of cutting-edge research and practical applications across a wide spectrum of fields. Featuring compact volumes of 50 to 125 pages, the series covers a range of content from professional to academic. Typical topics might include:

- A timely report of state-of-the art analytical techniques
- A bridge between new research results, as published in journal articles, and a contextual literature review
- A snapshot of a hot or emerging topic
- An in-depth case study or clinical example
- A presentation of core concepts that students must understand in order to make independent contributions

Briefs allow authors to present their ideas and readers to absorb them with minimal time investment. Briefs will be published as part of Springer's eBook collection, with millions of users worldwide. In addition, Briefs will be available for individual print and electronic purchase. Briefs are characterized by fast, global electronic dissemination, standard publishing contracts, easy-to-use manuscript preparation and formatting guidelines, and expedited production schedules. We aim for publication 8–12 weeks after acceptance. Both solicited and unsolicited manuscripts are considered for publication in this series.

More information about this series at http://www.springer.com/series/10028

Andrea Tagarelli • Roberto Interdonato

Mining Lurkers in Online Social Networks

Principles, Models, and Computational Methods

 Springer

Andrea Tagarelli
DIMES, Cubo 42C, Piano 5
University of Calabria
Arcavacata di Rende, Italy

Roberto Interdonato
UMR TETIS
CIRAD
Montpellier, France

ISSN 2191-5768   ISSN 2191-5776   (electronic)
SpringerBriefs in Computer Science
ISBN 978-3-030-00228-2   ISBN 978-3-030-00229-9   (eBook)
https://doi.org/10.1007/978-3-030-00229-9

Library of Congress Control Number: 2018955500

This Springer imprint is published by the registered company Springer Nature Switzerland AG
The registered company address is: Gewerbestrasse 11, 6330 Cham, Switzerland

Contents

Chapter 1
Introduction

Abstract This chapter opens the brief by introducing the readers to its research subject. The chapter provides main motivations and implications for studying a number of problems related to the theme of this brief, which will be elaborated in the subsequent eight chapters. The chapter also clarifies the target audience of scope of this brief, and finally provides acknowledgements.

Research in Web and network sciences has witnessed a large body of studies traditionally focusing on online users that take on either a "positive" or a "negative" role, i.e., influencers, experts, trendsetters, on the one side, and spammers, trolls, bogus users, on the other side. While the importance of studying these central figures has been widely recognized, less attention has been paid to the fact that all large-scale online social networks (OSNs) are characterized by a *participation inequality* principle. This principle is commonly expressed by a hypothetical "1:9:90" rule [1] stating that while only about 1% of users (which include influential users, opinion leaders, etc.) create the vast majority of social content, and another 9% are occasional contributors (i.e., they may post, comment, or like from time to time), the remaining 90% of users just observe ongoing discussions, read posts, watch videos, and so on. In other words, the real audience of OSNs does not actively contribute; rather, it takes on a *silent role*. Clearly, the actual proportions vary from network to network (e.g., [2, 4, 7]), but this disequilibrium between the niche of super contributors and the crowd of silent users is common to all large-scale OSNs.

As a fundamental premise, this kind of users should not be trivially regarded as totally inactive users, i.e., registered users who do not use their account to join the OSN. Actually, a silent user can be perceived as someone who gains benefit from others' information and services without giving back to the OSN. For this reason, such users are also called *lurkers*.

Understanding and mining lurkers is very arduous. The definition of lurker itself is multifaceted [5], as the meanings and interpretations of lurking may range from negative ones (e.g., lurkers might be seen as a menace for the cyberspace when they maliciously feed on others' intellects) to neutral (e.g., when they are seen as harmless and reflect a subjective reticence to actively join the OSN) to even positive interpretations (e.g., when lurking is recommended, especially to newcomers, in order to learn the etiquette of the OSN).

Regardless of how such users are perceived by the other (active) users, lurkers might hold potential in terms of *social capital*, because they acquire knowledge from the OSN: by observing the user-generated communications, they can become aware of the existence of different perspectives and may make use of these perspectives in order to form their own opinions, but never or rarely they will let other people know their value (e.g., ideas, expertise, opinions, etc.). Therefore, it might be desirable to make lurkers' social capital available to other users [3]. This would be accomplished through some mechanism of *delurking* of these users, i.e., by encouraging lurkers to more actively participate in the OSN life.

In the above depicted scenario, it should hence be clear that if we want to deeply understand the feelings of an online community, or in other terms, if we want to extract knowledge from the behavioral patterns of its users, then analyzing lurkers in the same way as we normally do for the active users would be totally unfair. Rather, it requires dealing with a wider spectrum of feelings, actions, latent or not, and reactions over time, bearing in mind the existence of a *wisdom of crowd* and the value of *diversity* in any social environment. The latter is responsible for a great part of the crowd's potential since:

> Large groups of people are smarter than an elite few, no matter how brilliant they are — better at solving problems, fostering innovation, coming to wise decisions, even predicting the future [6].

Lurking analysis has been long studied in social science and human-computer interaction fields. The interest on this topic has also grown over the last few years in social network analysis and mining, since the research outcomes can impact on different scenarios, ranging from social network marketing to education learning, from collaborative networks to recommender and trust systems, and any other networked environment that can benefit from a deep understanding of the informational needs of their users. There is in fact an emergence for computational models, learning methodologies and techniques that are capable of mining lurking behaviors and utilizing this knowledge in new techniques and applications in social science, network science, and other information science related fields.

This brief is aimed to bring order to the wealth of research studies that have contributed so far to shape our understanding on OSN lurking phenomena and to drive the development of computational approaches that can be effectively applied to answer questions related to lurking behaviors.

1.1   Organization of This Brief

The rest of this brief is organized into eight chapters. In Chap. 2, we introduce the reader to several aspects of interest to understand the lurking phenomenon. For this purpose, guided by main findings drawn from social science and human-computer interaction research, we discuss the different interpretations of lurking and related implications, the motivational factors underlying this kind of user behavior, and the main criteria to promote delurking.

Next, our focus is moved to research results that are more relevant in web search and ranking, network science, and data mining fields. In Chap. 3, we first introduce the topology-driven lurking definition, which is at the basis of existing lurker mining methods, then we present the class of **LurkerRank** algorithms and their time-aware extensions, which are designed to assign every user a score expressing the degree of lurking in the OSN; the chapter ends with the description of a learning-to-rank framework for lurker prediction and classification.

In Chap. 4, we discuss main remarks and findings raised from the experimental evaluations of lurker ranking methods conducted over several OSNs, such as Twitter, FriendFeed, Flickr, Instagram, and Google+. We discuss how the ranking results produced by **LurkerRank** are effective in identifying and characterizing users at different grades of lurking. We also point out that **LurkerRank** solutions are correlated with data-driven rankings based on empirical influence. Then, we provide an in-depth analysis of aspects related to the time dimension, which aims to unveil the behavior of lurkers and their relations with other users. More specifically, we address a number of important research questions, including comparison of lurkers with other types of users (inactive users, newcomers, active users), lurkers' responsiveness, evolution of lurking trends, and evolution of topical interests of lurkers.

To shed light on the pervasiveness of the notion of lurking in different domains, in Chap. 5 we provide example scenarios of lurking in two contexts, namely collaboration networks and trust networks. As regards collaboration networks, we focus on a parallel between lurkers and *vicarious learners*, i.e., users who take "non-expert" roles such as apprentices or advisees. We illustrate how to model a vicarious-learning-oriented collaboration network and we describe a method to identify and rank vicarious learners on it, namely **VLRank**. The second part of the chapter is devoted to the study of relations between lurkers and trustwor- thy/untrustworthy users. Through an analysis on who-trusts-whom networks and social media networks, we clarify to what extent the general perception of lurkers as *untrustworthy* users is appropriate or not.

Chapter 6 is dedicated to the delurking problem. We first provide an overview of research works focusing on user engagement methodologies to understand how users can be motivated to participate and contribute to the OSN life. We then concentrate on the presentation of algorithmic solutions to support the task of persuading lurkers to become active participants in their OSN, with emphasis on computational approaches based on influence propagation and maximization.

We investigate aspects related to the role of lurkers in *social boundary spanning* contexts in Chap. 7. In this regard, we study the relation between lurkers and OSN communities, discussing how the across-community boundary spanning capability of a user can relate with the role s/he may takes in the community, and to what extent lurkers match community-based *bridge* users. Moreover, we address the problem of *alternate lurker-contributor* behaviors in a multilayer OSN, which corresponds to complex behaviors that may take users having accounts in multiple OSN platforms.

In Chap. 8, we present a game-theoretic framework to model dynamics of lurkers, and their engagement. We describe the Lurker Game as a model for analyzing the transitions from a lurking to a non-lurking (i.e., active) user role, and vice versa, in terms of evolutionary game theory.

We provide concluding remarks in Chap. 9, and also highlight open issues related to lurking behavior analysis and mining, thus offering pointers for future research.

1.2 Audience and Scope

The expected audience of this brief is comprised of computer and network scientists, and in particular scholars and practitioners interested in social networks, web search and data mining, computational social science, human-computer interaction, and related fields that are concerned with issues in user behavioral analysis and social information filtering in online communities.

We argue that the scope of this brief is broad. Indeed, not only lurking phenomena represent a challenging problem in the area of *social network analysis and mining*, but understanding the motivational factors underlying lurking dynamics is also relevant to *user modeling*. At the same time, determining the main strategies to promote engagement of silent users (i.e., delurking) is related to how enhanced *personalization* of user access and *adaptation* of the design of web-based systems and their interfaces can improve users' experience. *Graph mining* provides essential tools that represent the backbone of many solutions to mining problems in OSNs, and hence is fundamental to the development of algorithms for searching, ranking and mining lurkers in a network. Lurking-oriented analysis of *influence propagation* is a key step to develop effective delurking frameworks. *Social media analysis* also represents a mandatory step when analyzing lurker profiles: even though the amount of content produced by a lurker can be relatively low, its analysis can help unveil the topics that are supposed to attract the lurkers' attention. Yet, in the *community detection* field, it is important to understand how lurkers, being more consumers than producers, can play the role of bridges between different communities. Furthermore, lurking dynamics can also be modeled through *evolutionary game theory*, developing cooperator-defector models which can help devise strategies to encourage cooperative behaviors.

1.3 Thanks

In the last few years, we have dedicated a significant part of our research time to the study of lurking behaviors in OSNs. This was a great research experience, which enabled us shed light on a phenomenon that was seldom considered in the computer science community. This has brought us to the development of innovative solutions for problems lying at the confluence of disciplines such as social science, human-computer interaction, network science, and computer science.

Luckily for us, our studies have been recognized in important venues in social network analysis and mining, knowledge and data engineering, social computing, user modeling, and related fields. Therefore, we wish to thank the scientific and editorial boards involved in the ACM, IEEE, and Springer conferences and journals, which handled the peer-reviewed evaluation processes and eventually accepted to publish our works. We also acknowledge Prof. V.S. Subrahmanian, which acted as Series Editor for this brief and whose early encouragement prompted us to be engaged with the writing, and Susan Lagerstrom-Fife, as our Senior Publishing Editor.

We are grateful to our academic friends for sharing with us the good and bad of experiencing research on this topic. Without their invaluable support, we would not have come a long way. In this respect, our sincere gratitude goes to Antonio Caliò, Marco Alberto Javarone, Diego Perna, and Chiara Pulice.

Last but not least, a most fond thank-you goes to our families, in particular: Andrea to Monica, Alessandro Giovanni, and Michela Sofia, and Roberto to Roberta, Girolamo, and Adelina. Without their backing and love, most of the inspiration and concentration for our research would have been lost.

Part of the research work that seeded this brief was supported by a grant of the PON 2014-2020 FESR "NextShop" project (n. F/050374/01-03/X32).

References

1. C. Arthur. What is the 1% rule? In *The guardian. UK: Guardian News and Media.* 2006.
2. M. Ebner and A. Holzinger. Lurking: An underestimated human-computer phenomenon. *IEEE Multimedia*, 12(4):70–75, 2005.
3. R. Farzan, J. Morris DiMicco, and B. Brownholtz. Mobilizing lurkers with a targeted task. In *Proc. Int. Conf. on Weblogs and Social Media (ICWSM)*, 2010.
4. B. Nonnecke and J. J. Preece. Lurker demographics: counting the silent. In *Proc. ACM Conf. on Human Factors in Computing Systems (CHI)*, pages 73–80, 2000.
5. N. Sun, P. P.-L. Rau, and L. Ma. Understanding lurkers in online communities: a literature review. *Computers in Human Behavior*, 38:110–117, 2014.
6. J. Surowiecki. *The Wisdom of Crowds: Why the Many are Smarter Than the Few and how Collective Wisdom Shapes Business, Economies, Societies, and Nations.* Doubleday, 2004.
7. T. van Mierlo. The 1% rule in four digital health social networks: An observational study. *Medical Internet Research*, 16(2), 2014.

Chapter 2
Background

Abstract This chapter summarizes main literature and relating findings from social science and human-computer interaction research, focusing on: the different interpretations of lurking and related implications, the motivational factors underlying this kind of user behavior, and the main criteria to promote delurking of lurkers.

2.1 Perception of Lurking

Lurkers are usually perceived in different ways from the other members of a community. Some of the studies considered lurkers to be selfish free-riders, thus conveying a negative attitude toward them [19, 24, 32, 42]. In effect, an important point is that the sustainability of an online community requires fresh content and timely interactions, and within this view lurkers are considered to just benefit from observing others' interaction and contribute little value to the community [40].

Most of studies however tend to have a non-negative interpretation of lurking. It has been shown in many works that lurkers are not free-riders [26, 27, 31], and that lurkers perceive themselves as community members [26]. Following the liberal model of democracy, lurking is considered as passive participation that permits inclusion [11]. Even more, in [7], lurking is reconsidered as an active, participative and valuable form of online behavior. Lurking has been often recognized as a form of cognitive apprenticeship known as *legitimate peripheral participation*. This perception is important to explain why lurking is normally welcome in online communities as it represents the natural form of learning the netiquette and social norms [21]. Other perceptions of lurking refer to individual information strategy of microlearning [17] and knowledge sharing barriers (e.g., interpersonal or technological barriers) [3]. Yet, lurking is seen as a necessary trade-off that comes with overall engagement and use of the OSN, which is related to individual motivation for interpersonal surveillance according to communication privacy management theory [5].

© The Author(s), under exclusive license to Springer Nature Switzerland AG 2018   7
A. Tagarelli, R. Interdonato, *Mining Lurkers in Online Social Networks*,
SpringerBriefs in Computer Science, https://doi.org/10.1007/978-3-030-00229-9_2

2.2   How to Identify Lurkers?

Lurker characterization has been a controversial issue, since the early sociological studies to the more recent works in human-computer interaction. Most studies agree in that there are two main features, namely *seldom posting* and *mostly reading contents*.

Several attempts have been made to set quantitative standards, even though the definitions provided are actually informal. That is, lurkers are those users who: "never post in an online community" [26], "post messages only once in a long while" [13], "provide no contribution during a 3-month period" [28], "publish at most four posts from the beginning, or never post in the last four months" [12].

Leshed [22] introduces *publicity* and *intensity* as the two dimensions of a participation pattern. Publicity expresses the degree of a member's exposure, and it can be seen as the ratio of public (i.e., posting) to non-public (i.e., reading) activities; intensity is instead measured as the frequency of total activities performed by a member. Within this view, lurkers tend to have higher intensity and lower publicity.

In [39, 41], where the common scenario is that of online learning platforms, the authors propose to classify lurkers into *passive* and *active* lurkers: the former only read for their use, while the latter spread the knowledge gained from the OSN to others, and apply such knowledge in organizational activities. Furthermore, Springer et al. [35] distinguish lurkers from *non-users*, which read news but have no interest in the user comments/discussions.

One might think that we can capitalize on the previously discussed criteria and generalize them to adequately detect lurkers, but nope! This is mainly because the size, topics and culture of the OSN can greatly influence the presence and behaviors of lurkers. In this regard, let's first move on to gain an insight into motivational factors that drive online participation of members in an OSN; this will be useful to explain the reasons for lurking and to eventually develop strategies for motivating posting. Later, in Sect. 2.5, we shall briefly overview main contributions from social science and human-computer interaction research, highlighting the emergence for the development of computational approaches to lurking behavior analysis.

2.3   Why Do Lurkers Act?

Sun et al. [36] proposed to organize the influencing factors of OSN users into four categories:

- *environmental influence*, i.e., group-identity, usability, reputation, and pro-sharing norms factors that affect the user's feeling of the community, thus influencing her/his willingness to contribute to the community;
- *individual factors*, which include personal characteristics, goals, desires, needs;
- *commitment factors*, which reflect the relationship between the users and the community in terms of affective, normative and continuance commitment bonds;

Table 2.1 *Why do lurkers lurk?* Main reasons according to the unified model of influencing factors proposed by Sun et al. [36]

Type of factor	Reasons
Environmental influence	Bad usability/interaction design
	Information overload
	Poor quality of the posted contents
	Low response rate and long response delay
	Low reciprocity
	"Don't know how to post"
	"Others respond the way I would"
	"Just reading/browsing is enough"
Personal	Introversion, bashfulness
	Lack of self-efficacy
	No need to post—only seeking for information
	Missing the opportunity to earn money
	Time constraints
Commitment	Low verbal and affective intimacy with others
	Lack of commitment to the community
	Fear making a commitment
	Unwillingness to spend too much time to maintain a commitment
Security concerns	Worrying about the violation of private information
	Perception of poor quality requirements of security

- *quality requirement factors*, which refer to the user's expectation of the community in terms of security, privacy, and reliability.

Table 2.1 summarizes the application of the aforementioned categorization to understand the main reasons behind lurking. Note that lurking may not only depend on a reticent attitude with respect to the purpose of joining the community, but also often lurkers do not realize the importance of contribution; this means that enhancing pro-sharing norms (i.e., norms that stimulate members to share their knowledge with others) would have a significant influence on lurkers. Moreover, lurking can also manifest itself as a reaction behavior when users are worried that their private information may be revealed or their security may be threatened by posting, therefore they may decide to lurk to protect themselves [29].

2.4 How to Promote Delurking?

While the main causes that explain lurking have been widely investigated, by contrast, few suggestions have been given about *how to turn lurkers into participants/contributors*. Delurking actions can be broadly categorized into four main types [36]: *external stimuli, encouragement to participate, guidance for newcomers, usability improvement*.

Social exchange theory resembles reward-based strategies that apply to traditional communities to promote participation. Rewards can be either tangible (e.g., financial assets, bonds) or intangible (e.g., access to restricted information). Another classification scheme is to distinguish between controlling rewards and informative rewards. In the former case, the community offers money or various forms of grants (e.g., badges) to its users for their contributions, so lurkers may begin to post to earn money or accumulate grants [2]. The latter case refers to offering something that has little value, but for which users may feel honored and appreciated.

Providing encouraging information to community members motivates them to participate in group activities, therefore helps to set up a pro-sharing norm and enhance users' commitment to the community. Encouraging information also helps to improve users' confidence in expressing themselves and to make them understand the necessity of their contribution to the community [16]. Encouraging information includes welcome statements, introduction of reward rules, support for browsing and praise for the moderator. For example, lurkers of a given sub-community developed around an entity of interest (e.g., a person, or theme) would welcome messages that highlight the key topics, social events that describe how to approach a discussion in a forum, or that introduce the role of forum moderators or team leaders.

Newcomers are likely to lurk for a while to learn the culture of the community. Directions from elder members can help newcomers to become familiar with the community as quickly as possible [30]. However, sustaining cooperation among newcomers in order to turn them into stable users is challenging as it might also inhibit communication with existing members [9]. In this regard, particular attention has been devoted to the design of personalized engagement strategies in different contexts, such as online communities for academic conferences [23] and community-based course recommender systems [8].

Also, the design of the OSN interface and related interaction experience can influence lurking behaviors. Therefore, OSN administrators should improve the usability and learnability of the system, making it easier for users to participate, especially for newcomers. For example, communities can simplify the procedures to send and respond messages. Moreover, in order to alleviate information overload, which is recognized as a major negative factor for participation, various mechanisms of information filtering could be applied, such as: recommending threads of discussion, providing visual maps of the categories of activities, recommending response messages [15].

2.5 Lurking as a Computational Problem

As previously introduced, there has been a great deal of attention to lurking analysis in social science and human-computer interaction research. Soroka and Rafaeli [34] investigate relations between lurking and cultural capital, i.e., a member's level of community-oriented knowledge. Cultural capital is found positively correlated with both the degree of active participation and, except for longer-time lurkers, with delurking. The studies in [6, 25] leverage the significance of conceptualizing the lurking roles in relation to their boundary spanning and knowledge brokering activities across multiple community engagement spaces. The study proposed in [4] raises the opportunity of rethinking of the nature of lurking from a group learning perspective, whereby the engagement of intentional lurkers is considered within the collective knowledge construction activity. The interactive/interpassive connotation of social media users' behavior is studied in [18] under a qualitative and grounded-theory-based approach. In the context of multiple online communities in an enterprise community service, lurking is found as only partially driven by the member's engagement but significantly affected by the member's disposition toward a topic, work task or social group [25]. Exploring epistemological motivations behind lurking dynamics is the main focus of the study in [33], which indeed reviews major relevant literature on epistemic curiosity in the context of online communities and provides a set of propositions on the propensity to lurk and delurk. Like in [6], this work mainly offers insights that might be useful to guide an empirical evaluation of lurkers' emotional traits. The study in [14] examines peripheral participation in Wikipedia, and designs a system to elicit lightweight editing contributions from Wikipedia readers.

A limitation common to all the aforementioned studies is that their main findings are drawn based on qualitative hypotheses and without being supported by computational learning approaches.

From this perspective, early work on lurking behaviors analysis recognized, explicitly or not, lurking as one of the roles users play through their life in the OSN. For instance, Anand et al. [1] relate the altruism of users to their level of capabilities, and indicate that the benefit derived from being altruistic is larger than that reaped by selfish users or free riders. Fazeen et al. [10] develop supervised classification methods for the various OSN actors, including lurkers, although leaving lurking cases out of experimental evaluation. Similarly, Lang and Wu [20] analyzed various factors that influence lifetime of OSN users, distinguishing between active and passive lifetime. While examining to what extent active and passive lifetime are correlated, the authors observed that the study of passive lifetime requires to know the user's last login date, which is however unavailable in many OSN platforms.

The lack of knowledge on the opportunity of modeling and mining lurking behaviors in OSNs was first filled by the studies in [37, 38]. In the following chapter, we shall present an overview of the developed computational approaches to characterize and rank lurkers in a OSN graph.

References

1. S. Anand, R. Chandramouli, K. P. Subbalakshmi, and M. Venkataraman. Altruism in social networks: good guys do finish first. *Social Netw. Analys. Mining*, 3(2):167–177, 2013.
2. A. Anderson, D. Huttenlocher, J. Kleinberg, and J. Leskovec. Steering user behavior with badges. In *Proc. ACM Conf. on World Wide Web (WWW)*, 2013.

3. A. Ardichvili. Learning and knowledge sharing in virtual communities of practice: motivators, barriers, and enablers. *Advances in Developing Human Resources*, 10:541–554, 2008.

4. F. C. Chen and H.-M. Chang. Do lurking learners contribute less?: a knowledge co-construction perspective. In *Proc. Conf. on Communities and Technologies (C&T)*, pages 169–178, 2011.

5. J. T. Child and S. C. Starcher. Fuzzy Facebook privacy boundaries: Exploring mediated lurking, vague-booking, and Facebook privacy management. *Computers in Human Behavior*, 54:483–490, 2016.

6. J. Cranefield, P. Yoong, and S. L. Huff. Beyond Lurking: The Invisible Follower-Feeder In An Online Community Ecosystem. In *Proc. Pacific Asia Conf. on Information Systems (PACIS)*, page 50, 2011.

7. N. Edelmann. Reviewing the definitions of "lurkers" and some implications for online research. *Cyberpsychology, Behavior, and Social Networking*, 16(9):645–649, 2013.

8. R. Farzan and P. Brusilovsky. Encouraging user participation in a course recommender system: An impact on user behavior. *Computers in Human Behavior*, 27(1):276–284, 2011.

9. R. Farzan and S. Han. My friends are here!: Why talk to "strangers"? In *Proc. ACM Conf. on Computer Supported Cooperative Work & Social Computing*, CSCW Companion '14, pages 161–164, 2014.

10. M. Fazeen, R. Dantu, and P. Guturu. Identification of leaders, lurkers, associates and spammers in a social network: context-dependent and context-independent approaches. *Social Netw. Analys. Mining*, 1(3):241–254, 2011.

11. M. M. Ferree, W. A. Gamson, J. Gerhards, and D. Rucht. *Shaping abortion discourse: Democracy and the public sphere in Germany and the United States*. Cambridge University Press, New York, 2002.

12. D. Ganley, C. Moser, and P. Groenewegen. Categorizing behavior in online communities: A look into the world of cake bakers. In *Proc. HICSS*, pages 3457–3466, 2012.

13. S. A. Golder and J. Donath. Social roles in electronic communities. *Internet Research*, 5:19–22, 2004.

14. A. Halfaker, O. Keyes, and D. Taraborelli. Making peripheral participation legitimate: reader engagement experiments in Wikipedia. In *Proc. ACM Conf. on Computer Supported Cooperative Work (CSCW)*, pages 849–860, 2013.

15. X. Han, W. Wei, C. Miao, J.-P. Mei, and H. Song. Context-Aware Personal Information Retrieval From Multiple Social Networks. *IEEE Computational Intelligence Magazine*, 9(2):18–28, 2014.

16. J. Imlawi and D. G. Gregg. Engagement in online social networks: The impact of self-disclosure and humor. *Int. J. Hum. Comput. Interaction*, 30(2):106–125, 2014.

17. N. Kahnwald and T. Köhler. Microlearning in virtual communities of practice? an explorative analysis of changing information behaviour. In *Proc. Microlearning Conf.*, pages 157–172, 2006.

18. K. E. Kappler and R. R. de Querol. Is there anybody out there? – social media as a new social fetish. In *Proc. ACM Web Science Conf. (WebSci)*, 2011.

19. P. Kollock and M. Smith. Managing the virtual commons. In *Computer-mediated communication: Linguistic, social, and cross-cultural perspectives*, pages 109–128. 1996.

20. J. Lang and S. F. Wu. Social network user lifetime. *Social Netw. Analys. Mining*, 3(3):285–297, 2013.

21. J. Lave and E. Wenger. *Situated Learning: Legitimate Peripheral Participation*. Cambridge University Press, 1991.

22. G. Leshed. Posters, lurkers, and in between: A multidimensional model of online community participation patterns. In *Proc. HIC*, 2005.

23. C. López, R. Farzan, and P. Brusilovsky. Personalized incremental users' engagement: driving contributions one step forward. In *Proc. ACM Int. Conf. on Support Group Work (GROUP)*, pages 189–198, 2012.

24. M. Morris and C. Ogan. The internet as mass medium. *Journal of Communication*, 46(1):39–50, 1996.

25. M. Muller. Lurking as personal trait or situational disposition: lurking and contributing in enterprise social media. In *Proc. ACM Conf. on Computer Supported Cooperative Work (CSCW)*, pages 253–256, 2012.

26. B. Nonnecke, D. Andrews, and J. J. Preece. Non-public and public online community participation: Needs, attitudes and behavior. *Electronic Commerce Research*, 6(1):7–20, 2006.

27. B. Nonnecke, J. Preece, D. Andrews, and R. Voutour. Online lurkers tell why. In *Proc. 10th Americas Conference on Information Systems (AMCIS)*, page 321, 2004.

28. B. Nonnecke and J. J. Preece. Lurker demographics: counting the silent. In *Proc. ACM Conf. on Human Factors in Computing Systems (CHI)*, pages 73–80, 2000.

29. B. Osatuyi. Is lurking an anxiety-masking strategy on social media sites? the effects of lurking and computer anxiety on explaining information privacy concern on social media platforms. *Computers in Human Behavior*, 49:324–332, 2015.

30. Z. Pan, Y. Lu, and S. Gupta. How heterogeneous community engage newcomers? The effect of community diversity on newcomers' perception of inclusion: An empirical study in social media service. *Computers in Human Behavior*, 39:100–111, 2014.

31. J. J. Preece, B. Nonnecke, and D. Andrews. The top five reasons for lurking: improving community experiences for everyone. *Computers in Human Behavior*, 20(2):201–223, 2004.

32. H. Rheingold. *The virtual community: Homesteading on the electronic frontier*. MIT Press, 2000.

33. A. Schneider, G. von Krogh, and P. Jager. "What's coming next?" Epistemic curiosity and lurking behavior in online communities. *Computers in Human Behavior*, 29:293–303, 2013.

34. V. Soroka and S. Rafaeli. Invisible participants: how cultural capital relates to lurking behavior. In *Proc. ACM Conf. on World Wide Web (WWW)*, pages 163–172, 2006.

35. N. Springer, I. Engelmann, and C. Pfaffinger. User comments: motives and inhibitors to write and read. *Information, Communication & Society*, 18(7):798–815, 2015.

36. N. Sun, P. P.-L. Rau, and L. Ma. Understanding lurkers in online communities: a literature review. *Computers in Human Behavior*, 38:110–117, 2014.

37. A. Tagarelli and R. Interdonato. "Who's out there?": Identifying and Ranking Lurkers in Social Networks. In *Proc. Int. Conf. on Advances in Social Networks Analysis and Mining (ASONAM)*, pages 215–222, 2013.

38. A. Tagarelli and R. Interdonato. Lurking in social networks: topology-based analysis and ranking methods. *Social Netw. Analys. Mining*, 4(230):27, 2014.

39. M. Takahashi, M. Fujimoto, and N. Yamasaki. The active lurker: Influence of an in-house online community on its outside environment. In *Proc. ACM SIGGROUP Conf. on Supporting Group Work*, pages 1–10, 2003.

40. T. van Mierlo. The 1% rule in four digital health social networks: An observational study. *Medical Internet Research*, 16(2), 2014.

41. B. Walker, J. Redmond, and A. Lengyel. Are they all the same? lurkers and posters on the net. *eCULTURE*, 3(1), 2013.

42. B. Wellman and M. Gulia. Net surfers don't ride alone: Virtual communities as communities. In *Networks in the Global Village*, pages 331–366. 1999.

Chapter 3
Characterization and Ranking of Lurkers

Abstract In this chapter, we discuss computational approaches to identify and rank lurkers in online social networks. We begin with a formal definition of topology-driven lurking and a detailed description of a family of centrality methods specifically conceived for ranking lurkers solely based on network topology, namely LurkerRank. To better model dynamics of user behaviors, the Time-Aware LurkerRank models are also described. The chapter ends with the description of a learning-to-rank framework for lurker prediction and classification.

One essential problem in web and network science is the identification of the nodes in a network that are important, or *central*, according to some reasonable criteria. While there is no unique interpretation of centrality, most of the research efforts have traditionally focused on definitions aiming at determining the node's status of being located in strategic locations within the network. The identification of the most central nodes in the network is a key-enabling task for further analysis [23].

Along the same line of thought, the authors in [20, 21] have brought for the first time the concept of centrality in the context of lurking behavior analysis. The goal was to define a *lurking scoring* function, and utilize this function to produce a ranking of users at different degrees of lurking.

Moreover, as for many well-known centrality methods (e.g., PageRank) that were originally conceived for ranking nodes based solely on their location in the network, analogously the lurker ranking algorithms were defined by only requiring the topology information of the social network graph. Let's now introduce the topology-driven lurking definition, which is at the basis of existing lurker ranking methods.

3.1 Topology-Driven Lurking Definition

It is a common assumption that user interactions in an OSN are naturally modeled as influence relationships, as these are used to identify and rank influential users. The conventional ranking model is indeed an influence graph, whereby node relations are

A. Tagarelli, R. Interdonato, *Mining Lurkers in Online Social Networks*,
SpringerBriefs in Computer Science, https://doi.org/10.1007/978-3-030-00229-9_3

modeled such that the more (or more relevant) incoming links a node has the more important it is—for instance, the more followers a user has, the more interesting his/her posted contents might be. This is nothing more that the measure of degree centrality, and also one of the key aspects in the classic PageRank [4] model and related eigenvector centrality measures [23]. However, as was first studied in the context of adversarial information retrieval (e.g., spam detection [10]), the in-degree of a node can easily be affected by malicious manipulation, and hence the number of incoming links is not to be trusted as unique estimator of the node's importance score. Rather, as discussed in [8] in the Twitter scenario, the follower-to-followee ratio should in principle be considered, that is, if the number of followers exceeds those of followees then the user is likely to be an opinion-maker, otherwise her/his tweets are not that interesting. Moreover, it should be noted that classic influence-oriented centrality methods like PageRank cannot be directly applied to explain lurking behaviors, since they assume that node relations follow the flow of influence propagation, which is related to the *amount of information a node produces*. By contrast, lurking behaviors build on the *amount of information a node consumes*; intuitively, if user v follows user u, then v is likely to benefit from receiving (i.e., consuming) content produced by u.

Based on the above assumption, the authors in [20, 21] provide a definition of lurking that aims to lay out the essential hypotheses of a lurking status based solely on the topology information available in an OSN.

Let $\mathscr{G} = \langle \mathscr{V}, \mathscr{E} \rangle$ denote the directed graph representing an OSN, with set of nodes (members) $\mathscr{V}$ and set of edges $\mathscr{E}$, whereby the semantics of any edge (u, v) is that v is consuming information produced by u. A node v with infinite in/out-degree ratio (i.e., a sink node) is trivially regarded as a lurker. A node v with in/out-degree ratio not below 1 shows a lurking status, whose strength is determined based on [20, 21]:

> **Principle I: Overconsumption**. The excess of information-consumption over information-production. The strength of v's lurking status is proportional to its in/out-degree ratio.
>
> **Principle II: Authoritativeness of the Information Received**. The valuable amount of information received from its in-neighbors. The strength of v's lurking status is proportional to the influential (non-lurking) status of the v's in-neighbors.
>
> **Principle III: Non-authoritativeness of the Information Produced**. The non-valuable amount of information sent to its out-neighbors. The strength of v's lurking status is proportional to the lurking status of the v's out-neighbors.

Figure 3.1 shows a schematic illustration of the bow-tie-like structure of the portion of an OSN involving lurkers. The figure depicts the relation between the component of the higher-authoritativeness bandwidth of the incoming information (i.e., consumed by lurkers) and of the lower-authoritativeness flow of outgoing information (i.e., produced by lurkers) with the portion of OSN comprised of lurkers. In accord with the three-principle definition of lurking previously presented, the "knot" of lurkers has a larger "bow" that corresponds to the information-consumption flow.

Fig. 3.1 Unbalanced bow-tie picture providing a high-level view of the lurkers' portion of an OSN, based on the three-principle definition of lurking in [20, 21]

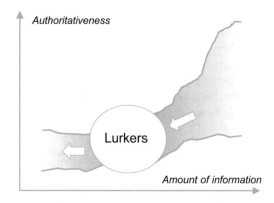

Note that, for the sake of simplicity of illustration, the proportions are arbitrary and connectivity considerations about nodes in the network are discarded.

3.2   The LurkerRank Family of Ranking Algorithms

The three-principle definition of lurking in [20, 21] forms the basis for three ranking models that differently account for the contributions of a node's in-neighborhood and out-neighborhood.

According to Principle I, a basic way of scoring a node as a lurker is by means of its in/out-degree ratio. However, this way has clearly the disadvantage of assigning many nodes the same or very close ranks and, as we previously discussed, it ignores that the status of both the in-neighbors (Principle II) and out-neighbors (Principle III) contributes to the status of any given node. In the following we elaborate on each of those aspects separately.

The first model is called *in-neighbors-driven lurking*, and is defined such that the score of a node increases with the number of its in-neighbors and with their likelihood of being non-lurkers (i.e., relatively high out/in-degree); moreover, the model involves a factor inversely proportional to the node's out-degree accounting for its own in/out-degree property. Let $N^{in}(v)$ and $N^{out}(v)$ denote the set of in-neighbors and out-neighbors, respectively, for any node $v \in \mathcal{V}$. Formally, the in-neighbors-driven lurking score of node $v \in \mathcal{V}$ is defined as [20, 21]:

$$\mathscr{L}_{in}(v) = \frac{1}{|N^{out}(v)|} \sum_{u \in N^{in}(v)} \frac{|N^{out}(u)|}{|N^{in}(u)|} \mathscr{L}_{in}(u) \tag{3.1}$$

The contribution of out-neighbors for the calculation of a node's lurking score, according to Principle III, is captured in the *out-neighbors-driven lurking* model. Here, the lurking score of a node increases with the tendency of its out-neighbors of being lurkers. More specifically, the model contains a functional term that is proportional to the sum of the in/out ratio of each of the node's out-neighbors. The intuition here is that this functional term is useful to capture possible cases of linkage between users showing a certain lurking status, though their provision of information is expected to be relatively poor. However, to avoid propagating the lurking status from actual lurkers to the (non-lurker) nodes from which the information is received, another functional term is introduced to penalize the node's score if it receives less than what its out-neighbors receive [20, 21]:

$$\mathscr{L}_{\text{out}}(v) = \frac{|N^{in}(v)|}{\sum_{u \in N^{out}(v)} |N^{in}(u)|} \sum_{u \in N^{out}(v)} \frac{|N^{in}(u)|}{|N^{out}(u)|} \mathscr{L}_{\text{out}}(u) \tag{3.2}$$

All three principles are also integrated into a unified lurking model, called *in-out-neighbors-driven lurking* [20, 21]:

$$\mathscr{L}_{\text{inout}}(v) = \left(\frac{1}{|N^{out}(v)|} \sum_{u \in N^{in}(v)} \frac{|N^{out}(u)|}{|N^{in}(u)|} \mathscr{L}_{\text{inout}}(u) \right)$$

$$\left(1 + \left(\frac{|N^{in}(v)|}{\sum_{u \in N^{out}(v)} |N^{in}(u)|} \sum_{u \in N^{out}(v)} \frac{|N^{in}(u)|}{|N^{out}(u)|} \mathscr{L}_{\text{inout}}(u) \right) \right) \tag{3.3}$$

In the above equation, the aspect related to the strength of non-lurking behavior of in-neighbors is emphasized, since it is expected to have a better fit of the hypothetical likelihood function—indeed, this has been widely demonstrated in the extensive experimental evaluation described in [20, 21].

Note that, in all the above equations, the cardinality values of set functions $N^{in}(\cdot)$ and $N^{out}(\cdot)$ are Laplace add-one smoothed, clearly to prevent zero or infinite ratios.

A complete specification of the lurker ranking models has been provided in terms of two well-known eigenvector centrality approaches, namely *PageRank* [4] and *alpha-centrality* [3]. For instance, the following equation provides the PageRank-based in-neighbors-driven LurkerRank score for any node v, denoted as $LR_{\text{in}}(v)$ [20, 21]:

$$LR_{\text{in}}(v) = d \left(\frac{1}{|N^{out}(v)|} \sum_{u \in N^{in}(v)} \frac{|N^{out}(u)|}{|N^{in}(u)|} \right) LR_{\text{in}}(u) + (1-d)p(v) \tag{3.4}$$

where $p(v)$ denotes the value for v in the personalization (or teleportation) vector, which is by default set to $1/|\mathcal{V}|$, and d is a damping factor ranging within [0,1], usually set to 0.85.

It has been shown that both the PageRank-based and the alpha-centrality-based LurkerRank methods reach ranking stability quickly, with the latter being slightly faster the former however at the cost of lower diversification of the ranking scores [21].

3.3   Time-Aware LurkerRank Algorithms

Online social environments are highly dynamic systems, as individuals join, participate, attract, cooperate, and disappear over time. This clearly affects the shape of the OSN both in terms of its social (followship) and interaction graphs [2, 5, 7, 11, 13, 15, 16, 24]. Moreover, everybody agrees on the stance that users normally look for the most updated information, therefore the timeliness of users and their relations become essential for evaluation [1, 12, 14, 18, 25, 26]. Like any other user, lurkers as well may be interested not only in the authoritative sources of information, but also in the timely sources.

Research on temporal network analysis and mining strives to understand the driving forces behind the evolution of OSNs and what dynamical patterns are produced by an interplay of various user-related dimensions in OSNs. Dealing with the temporal dimension to mine lurkers appears to be even more challenging. Yet, it's also an emergent necessity, as users in an OSN naturally evolve playing different roles, showing a stronger or weaker tendency toward lurking at different times. Moreover, as temporal dimension in an OSN is generally examined in terms of online frequency of the users, it's important to take into account that lurkers may have unusual frequency of online presence as well as unusual frequency of interaction with other users.

In this section we refer to the study in [22] in which the authors extend the LurkerRank algorithms to account for the temporal dimension when determining the lurking scores of users in the network. Two approaches are proposed based on different models of temporal network:

- *Transient ranking*, i.e., a measure of a user's lurking score based on a time-static (snapshot) graph model;
- *Cumulative ranking*, i.e., a measure of a user's lurking score that encompasses a given time interval (sequence of snapshots), based on a time-evolving graph model.

3.3.1   Freshness and Activity Trend

The building blocks of the time-aware LurkerRank methods rely on the specification of two temporal aspects of interest, namely *freshness* and *activity trend*, both at user and at user relation level.

Users in the network are assumed to perform actions and interact with each other over a timespan $\mathscr{T} \subseteq \mathbb{T}$. the time-varying graph of an OSN is seen as a discrete time system, i.e., the time is discretized at a fixed granularity (e.g., day, week, month).

User freshness function takes into account the timestamps of the latest information produced (i.e., posted) by a user, where higher values correspond to more recent activities of the user within the temporal interval of interest. Given a temporal subset $T \subseteq \mathcal{T}$, being in interval notation of the form $T = [t_s, t_e]$, with $t_s \leq t_e$, the *freshness function* $\varphi_T(t)$ for any time t has values within $[0, 1]$ and is defined as [22]:

$$\varphi_T(t) = \begin{cases} 1/\log_2(2 + (t_e - t)), & \text{if } t \in T \\ 0, & \text{otherwise.} \end{cases} \tag{3.5}$$

Given a user u, let T_u be the set of time units at which u performed actions in the network. The *freshness* of u at a given temporal subset of interest T is defined as [22]:

$$f_T(u) = \max\{\varphi_T(t), \ t \in T_u \text{ s.t. } t_s \leq t \leq t_e\} \tag{3.6}$$

Higher values of $f_T(u)$ correspond to more recent activities of u w.r.t. T.

Analogously, the timestamps of the latest information consumed by a user are considered in relation to another user's actions, so that the freshness of interaction between two users over the time interval of interest corresponds to the maximum freshness over the sequence of pairs production/consumption timings.

The second aspect considered by the authors in [22] is the activity trend of a user, which models how the users' posting actions vary over time. The time series corresponding to the activities of a user is suitably processed in order to capture the significant variations in the time series profile. Formally, each time series $S_u = [(x_1, t_1), \ldots, (x_n, t_n)]$, which represents the number of actions performed by user u at each time $t \in T_u$, is subject to the *Derivative time series Segment Approximation* (DSA) [9]. DSA produces a new series of h values, with $h \ll n$, through derivative estimation, segmentation and approximation steps. The resulting DSA series $\mathcal{T}_u$ has the form $\mathcal{T}_u = [(\alpha_1, t_1), \ldots \ldots, (\alpha_h, t_h)]$, such that $\alpha_j = \arctan(\mu(s_j))$ and $t_j = t_{j-1} + l_j$, with $j = [1..h]$, where s_j is the j-th segment, l_j its length, and $\mu(s_j)$ the mean of its points. Upon normalization of the α values in $\mathcal{T}_u$, the *activity trend* of user u over T_u is defined as the time sequence:

$$a(u) = [(\hat{\alpha}_1, t_1), \ldots, (\hat{\alpha}_h, t_h)] \tag{3.7}$$

Therefore, given a specific subinterval $T \subseteq T_u$, the activity trend of u w.r.t. T corresponds to the subsequence $a_T(u)$ of $a(u)$ that fits T. Moreover, the *average activity* of u over T, denoted by $\overline{a_T}(u)$, is defined as the average of the $\hat{\alpha}$ values within $a_T(u)$.

Analogously, the activity trend of interaction is modeled on the basis of the time series of responsive actions from one user with respect to the posting of another user.

3.3.2 Time-Static LurkerRank

The time-static LurkerRank proposed in [22] is designed to work on a subset of relational data that are restricted to a particular subinterval of the network timespan, i.e., a single snapshot of the temporal network. The freshness and activity functions are used to define a time-aware weighting scheme that determines both the strength of the productivity of a user and the strength of the interaction between any two users linked at a given time. Two real-valued, non-negative coefficients ω_f, ω_a are introduced to control the importance of the freshness and the activity trend in the weighting scheme. Given a temporal interval of interest T, and coefficients ω_f, ω_a, the function $w_T(\cdot)$ is defined in terms of the user freshness and average activity calculated for any user $v \in \mathcal{V}$ [22]:

$$w_T(v) = \begin{cases} \frac{\omega_f f_T(v) + \omega_a \overline{a_T}(v)}{\omega_f + \omega_a}, & \text{if } f_T(v) \neq 0, \overline{a_T}(v) \neq 0 \\ f_T(v), & \text{if } f_T(v) \neq 0, \overline{a_T}(v) = 0 \\ 1, & \text{otherwise} \end{cases} \quad (3.8)$$

By default, the two coefficients are set uniformly as $\omega_f = \omega_a = 0.5$. If T_u is contained into T (i.e., $f_T(v) \neq 0$) and the average activity is zero, the w_T value will coincide to the freshness value, which is strictly positive; otherwise, if $f_T(v) = 0$, the w_T value will equal one. Moreover, w_T is equal to 1 if either the freshness and average activity are maximum or T is not relevant to the timespan over which the user has been active.

Analogously to $w_T(\cdot)$, the function $w_T(\cdot, \cdot)$ is defined in terms of the freshness and average activity of interaction calculated for any $u, v \in \mathcal{V}$ such that $(u, v) \in \mathcal{E}$, as follows [22]:

$$w_T(u, v) = \begin{cases} \frac{\omega_f f_T(u,v) + \omega_a \overline{a_T}(u,v)}{\omega_f + \omega_a}, & \text{if } f_T(u, v) \neq 0, \\ & \overline{a_T}(u, v) \neq 0 \\ f_T(u, v), & \text{if } f_T(u, v) \neq 0, \\ & \overline{a_T}(u, v) = 0 \\ 0, & \text{otherwise} \end{cases} \quad (3.9)$$

The *time-static LurkerRank* method, denoted as Ts-LR, involves the above functions $w_T(\cdot)$ and $w_T(\cdot, \cdot)$. The method shares with the basic LurkerRank formulation the way the in-neighbors-driven lurking term is combined with the out-neighbors-driven lurking term, that is, for any user $v \in \mathcal{V}$ and temporal interval of interest T [22]:

$$Ts\text{-}LR_T(v) = d[\mathcal{L}_{\text{in}}(v)(1 + \mathcal{L}_{\text{out}}(v))] + (1 - d)/(|\mathcal{V}|) \quad (3.10)$$

To define the two terms in the above equation, the rationale behind the use of w_T assigned to each node v is to add a multiplicative factor that is inversely (resp. directly) proportional, otherwise neutral, to the size of the in-neighborhood $N^{in}(()v)$ (resp. size of the out-neighborhood $N^{out}(()v)$) in the formulation of time-static LurkerRank algorithm. Therefore, the in-neighbors-driven lurking function $\mathscr{L}_{in}(v)$ is defined as [22]:

$$\mathscr{L}_{in}(v) = \frac{1}{w(v)|N^{out}(()v)|} \exp\left(- \sum_{u \in N^{in}(()v)} w(u, v)\right)$$

$$\sum_{u \in N^{in}(()v)} \frac{|N^{out}(()u)|}{|N^{in}(()u)|} Ts\text{-}LR_T(u) \qquad (3.11)$$

and the out-neighbors-driven lurking function $\mathscr{L}_{out}(v)$ as [22]:

$$\mathscr{L}_{out}(v) = \frac{|N^{in}(()v)|}{w(v) \sum_{u \in N^{out}(()v)} |N^{in}(()u)|} \exp\left(- \sum_{u \in N^{out}(()v)} w(v, u)\right)$$

$$\sum_{u \in N^{out}(()v)} \frac{|N^{in}(()u)|}{|N^{out}(()u)|} Ts\text{-}LR_T(u) \qquad (3.12)$$

Note that in the above equations, for the sake of simplicity, the subscript T are omitted in the freshness and activity trend functions, in the weighting function as well as in the set cardinality functions, since the reference interval of interest T is assumed clear from the context.

3.3.3 Time-Evolving LurkerRank

The time-static LurkerRank refers to a simple, single-snapshot temporal graph model. One issue is that information on the sequence of events concerning users' (re)actions may be lost as relations are aggregated into a single snapshot. To overcome this issue, the authors in [22] also define an alternative formulation of time-aware LurkerRank that is able to model, for each user v, the potential accumulated over a time-window of the contribution that each in-neighbor had to the computation of the lurking score of v.

First, the authors provide definitions for cumulative freshness and activity functions. These share as a template the analytical form determined by a cumulative scoring function $(g_{\leq})$ which, for any time $t \in T$, aggregates all values of a function g (defined in T) computed at times $t' \in \mathscr{T}$ less than or equal to t, following an exponential-decay model:

$$g_{\leq}(t) \propto g(t) + \sum_{t' < t}(1 - 2^{t'-t})g(t') \qquad (3.13)$$

Suppose the timespan $\mathcal{T}$ of the network is partitioned in consecutive sub-intervals $T_1, T_2, \ldots, T_i, \ldots = [t_0, t_1], (t_1, t_2], \ldots, (t_{i-1}, t_i] \ldots$. If t_i corresponds to the end-time of the span of interest whose latest sub-interval is T_i, the *cumulative user-freshness* function applied to user u is defined as to integrate (with exponential decay) all user-freshness values individually obtained at each sub-interval preceding t_i [22]:

$$cf_{T_i}(u) = f_{T_i}(u) + \sum_{t_k < t_i}(1 - 2^{t_k - t_i})f_{T_k}(u) \qquad (3.14)$$

Analogously, for each user u, the *cumulative user-activity* function is defined as [22]:

$$ca_{T_i}(u) = \overline{a_{T_i}}(u) + \sum_{t_k < t_i}(1 - 2^{t_k - t_i})\overline{a_{T_k}}(u) \qquad (3.15)$$

The definitions of cumulative freshness of interaction, $cf_{T_i}(u, v)$, and cumulative activity of interaction, $ca_{T_i}(u, v)$, at each T_i, and for every $(u, v) \in \mathcal{E}$, follow intuitions analogous to Eqs. (3.14) and (3.15), respectively.

The values yielded by the above defined four functions of cumulative freshness and activity, at user as well as at interaction level, are then normalized and multiplied by the corresponding information in the transient model [22]:

$$cf_{T_i}'(u) = \frac{cf_{T_i}(u)}{\max_j cf_{T_j}(u)} f_{T_i}(u) \qquad (3.16)$$

$$ca_{T_i}'(u) = \frac{ca_{T_i}(u)}{\max_j ca_{T_j}(u)} \overline{a_{T_i}}(u) \qquad (3.17)$$

The user-interaction function counterparts have analogous form to Eqs. (3.16) and (3.17). Intuitively, the freshness/activity information cumulated through times preceding a target time T_i will be valued w.r.t. the actual contribution (in terms of freshness/activity) that the user provides in the OSN at given time T_i.

The *time-evolving LurkerRank* method, denoted as Te-LR, follows a formula that is analogous to Ts-LR, while adopting new weighting functions, denoted as $cw_T(\cdot)$ and $cw_T(\cdot, \cdot)$, which have the following properties [22]:

- they have analytical form that is identical to $w_T(\cdot)$, given in Eq. (3.8), and $w_T(\cdot, \cdot)$, given in Eq. (3.9), respectively;
- they are defined, at user level, in terms of the functions $cf_{T_i}'(\cdot)$ and $ca_{T_i}'(\cdot)$ (given in Eqs. (3.16) and (3.17)), and at user-interaction level, in terms of the functions $cf_{T_i}'(\cdot, \cdot)$ and $ca_{T_i}'(\cdot, \cdot)$.

3.4   Learning to Rank Lurkers

LurkerRank methods and their time-aware extensions adopt a query-independent, eigen-vector-centrality based approach that utilizes the link graph structure underlying user relationships (e.g., followships, like/comment interactions).

Despite the meaningfulness and effectiveness of such methods, as we shall discuss in Chap. 4, the complexity of lurking behaviors hints at the opportunity of using any available, possibly *platform-specific*, information on the activity and interaction of lurkers in an OSN. Within this view, the study in [19] addresses the following research questions:

- Can we incorporate into a lurker ranking model various "signals" that can be used as behavioral features, upon which the evaluation of the degree of lurking of any user w.r.t. a given context (i.e., online environment) is performed?
- Can we enable a lurker ranking model to accurately be tuned by exploiting past lurking experiences?
- What if information on lurking behaviors is available from populations of different networks?
- Can we predict the lurking behavior of a previously unexamined user by avoiding to rank from scratch all users?

To answer the above questions, the authors in [19] define a machine-learning-based ranking, a.k.a. *learning-to-rank* (LTR), framework for the analysis of lurking behaviors. As in traditional ranking functions, a partial ordering (ranking) is provided for a set of objects, according to their degree of relevance to a given query. However, in LTR, the ranking function is learned from *training data* given in the form of ⟨*query, object, relevance label*⟩ tuples.

As one of the key technologies for modern web search, retrieval and personalization [6, 17], LTR adopts a supervised approach to learn from past user experiences. In the context of lurking behaviors, such historical data correspond to user tuples annotated according to the degree of lurking behavior. LTR training is accomplished according to a set of features which, being possibly of different types, would capture different aspects that can be useful predictors of lurking behaviors. Therefore, LTR can be seen as a helpful tool to handle cases where it would be difficult to gather sufficient and significant lurking information from the graph of user relationships.

Moreover, LTR allows for leveraging information from multiple OSNs to build a single ranking model. In fact, by treating multiple OSN platforms as different queries and building an LTR model from instances (users) that belong to the various platforms, lurker ranking results can be compared through different OSNs, thus *generalizing the concept of lurking to multiple networks*. Yet, LTR offers unprecedented opportunities for *incremental lurking scenarios*: once train-ed an LTR model, this can be used to assign any previously unobserved user with a lurking score, thus avoiding the calculation from scratch of a ranking scheme over the entire OSN graph.

The authors in [19] define the first *learning-to-lurker-rank* framework, dubbed **LTLR**, which exploits the unsupervised LurkerRank method to derive binary or graded relevance labels, and a feature engineering phase that accounts for relational (i.e., topology-based), media-based, activity rate, and platform-specific information on the commitment and interaction of users from different OSNs. *Relational* features correspond to local properties of a node in a graph, according to the three principles at the basis of the topology-driven lurking model previously discussed. Therefore, relational features include information about a node's in-neighbors, out-neighbors, and their ratio. *Media-based* features describe actions that a user performed or underwent in relation to her/his media in the OSN (e.g., posts, images). These are organized based on whether an action was perceived as manifestation of a user's active participation or passive participation. More in detail, media-based features can refer to *latent* actions (e.g., views/clicks) and *visible* actions; the latter, in turn, can be divided into *least-effort* actions (e.g., likes, favorites, mentions), and *most-effort* actions (e.g., comments, replies). *Activity rate* features are aimed to capture temporal aspects of a user's activity, in terms of frequency as well as latency [22]. Therefore, features of this type are expected to include information about the length of the time period between two temporally consecutive actions, or the average frequency of media created, or latent/least-/most-effort actions performed. Finally, *platform-specific* features regard indicators of the degree of a user's commitment and engagement to the social life in the online platform; for instance, information on badges or other forms of rewards for the user, the number of lists a user belongs to, or the length of time period for intensively active contribution.

Figure 3.2 shows the main modules and data flows in the **LTLR** framework. Note that the framework exploits information from multiple social media sources, such as Twitter, Instagram, GitHub, StackOverlflow, from which four types of features

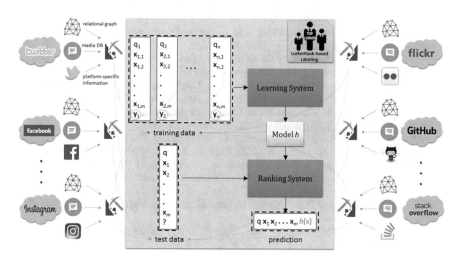

Fig. 3.2 Learning-to-lurker-rank (LTLR) framework [19]

are extracted and processed to build the feature space for the representation of the training data. Each of the training data instances is annotated with a relevance label expressing the degree of lurking of the corresponding user (module LurkerRank-based labeling, on the top-right corner of the internal box shown in the figure). Results obtained on 23 network datasets, which were built from 7 OSNs, have shown the significance of the LTLR approach, confirming the effectiveness of the LTR paradigm for ranking lurking behaviors. In particular, LTR methods such as LambdaMART and Coordinate Ascent can optimally predict the correct rank on test data even with few media-based, activity-rate or platform-specific features. A general trend is that a combination between relational and additional features should nonetheless be used to improve accuracy and ranking performance.

References

1. K. Berberich, M. Vazirgiannis, and G. Weikum. Time-Aware Authority Ranking. *Internet Mathematics*, 2(3):301–332, 2005.
2. M. Berlingerio, M. Coscia, F. Giannotti, A. Monreale, and D. Pedreschi. Evolving networks: Eras and turning points. *Intelligent Data Analysis*, 17(1):27–48, 2013.
3. P. Bonacich and P. Lloyd. Eigenvector-like measures of centrality for asymmetric relations. *Social Networks*, 23:191–201, 2001.
4. S. Brin and L. Page. The anatomy of a large-scale hypertextual Web search engine. *Computer Networks and ISDN Systems*, 30(1-7):107–117, 1998.
5. Ceren Budak, Divyakant Agrawal, and Amr El Abbadi. Structural trend analysis for online social networks. *Proceedings of the VLDB Endowment*, 4(10):646–656, 2011.
6. S. Chakrabarti. Learning to Rank in Vector Spaces and Social Networks. *Internet Mathematics*, 4(1–3):267–298, 2007.
7. Pasquale De Meo, Emilio Ferrara, Fabian Abel, Lora Aroyo, and Geert-Jan Houben. Analyzing user behavior across social sharing environments. *ACM Trans. on Intelligent Systems and Technology*, 5(1), 2013.
8. D. Gayo-Avello. Nepotistic relationships in Twitter and their impact on rank prestige algorithms. *Inf. Process. Manage.*, 49(6):1250–1280, 2013.
9. F. Gullo, G. Ponti, A. Tagarelli, and S. Greco. A time series representation model for accurate and fast similarity detection. *Pattern Recognition*, 42(11):2998–3014, 2009.
10. Z. Gyöngyi, H. Garcia-Molina, and J. O. Pedersen. Combating Web Spam with TrustRank. In *Proc. Int. Conf. on Very Large Data Bases (VLDB)*, pages 576–587, 2004.
11. Hawoong Jeong, Zoltan Néda, and Albert-László Barabási. Measuring preferential attachment in evolving networks. *EPL (Europhysics Letters)*, 61(4):567, 2003.
12. J. Jiang, C. Wilson, X. Wang, W. Sha, P. Huang, Y. Dai, and B. Y. Zhao. Understanding latent interactions in online social networks. *ACM Trans. on the Web*, 7(4):18, 2013.
13. R. Kumar, J. Novak, and A. Tomkins. Structure and evolution of online social networks. In *Proc. ACM SIGKDD Int. Conf. on Knowledge Discovery and Data Mining (KDD)*, pages 611–617, 2006.
14. J. Lang and S. F. Wu. Social network user lifetime. *Social Netw. Analys. Mining*, 3(3):285–297, 2013.
15. Janette Lehmann, Bruno Gonçalves, José J Ramasco, and Ciro Cattuto. Dynamical classes of collective attention in Twitter. In *Proc. ACM Conf. on World Wide Web (WWW)*, pages 251–260, 2012.

16. Jure Leskovec, Lars Backstrom, and Jon Kleinberg. Meme-tracking and the dynamics of the news cycle. In *Proc. ACM SIGKDD Int. Conf. on Knowledge Discovery and Data Mining (KDD)*, pages 497–506. ACM, 2009.

17. Tie-Yan Liu. *Learning to Rank for Information Retrieval*. Springer, 2011.

18. J. O'Madadhain and P. Smyth. EventRank: a framework for ranking time-varying networks. In *Proc. KDD Workshop on Link Discovery*, pages 9–16, 2005.

19. Diego Perna, Roberto Interdonato, and Andrea Tagarelli. Learning to lurker rank: an evaluation of learning-to-rank methods for lurking behavior analysis. *Social Netw. Analys. Mining*, 8(1):39:1–39:21, 2018.

20. A. Tagarelli and R. Interdonato. "Who's out there?": Identifying and Ranking Lurkers in Social Networks. In *Proc. Int. Conf. on Advances in Social Networks Analysis and Mining (ASONAM)*, pages 215–222, 2013.

21. A. Tagarelli and R. Interdonato. Lurking in social networks: topology-based analysis and ranking methods. *Social Netw. Analys. Mining*, 4(230):27, 2014.

22. A. Tagarelli and R. Interdonato. Time-aware analysis and ranking of lurkers in social networks. *Social Netw. Analys. Mining*, 5(1):23, 2015.

23. S. Wasserman and K. Faust. *Social Networks Analysis: Methods and Applications*. Cambridge University Press, 1994.

24. C. Wilson, A. Sala, K. P. N. Puttaswamy, and B. Y. Zhao. Beyond Social Graphs: User Interactions in Online Social Networks and their Implications. *ACM Trans. on the Web*, 6(4):17, 2012.

25. P. S. Yu, X. Li, and B. Liu. On the temporal dimension of search. In *Proc. ACM Conf. on World Wide Web (WWW)*, pages 448–449, 2004.

26. M Zignani, S. Gaito, G. P. Rossi, X. Zhao, H. Zheng, and B. Y. Zhao. Link and triadic closure delay: Temporal metrics for social network dynamics. In *Proc. Int. Conf. on Weblogs and Social Media (ICWSM)*, 2014.

Chapter 4
Lurking Behavior Analysis

Abstract In this chapter, we discuss main remarks and findings raised from the experimental evaluations of lurker rank methods conducted over several real-world OSNs, such as Twitter, FriendFeed, Flickr, Instagram, and Google+. We discuss how the ranking results produced by LurkerRank are effective in identifying and characterizing users at different grades of lurking. We also point out that LurkerRank solutions are correlated with data-driven rankings based on empirical influence. Then, we provide an in-depth analysis of aspects related to the time dimension, which aims to unveil the behavior of lurkers and their relations with other users. More specifically, we address a number of important research questions, including comparison of lurkers with other types of users (inactive users, newcomers, active users), lurkers' responsiveness, evolution of lurking trends, and evolution of topical interests of lurkers.

4.1 Significance and Effectiveness of LurkerRank

The LurkerRank methods described in Chap. 3 have been used in a number of research works, starting with [7–9]. In this regard, the methods have been experimentally evaluated, using several OSNs of different types, such as Twitter, FriendFeed, Flickr, Instagram, and Google+ network datasets.

Due to the novelty of the lurking behavior analysis problem from a computational perspective, at the time of the aforementioned early works, a major issue that the authors had to deal with was the lack of ground-truth or benchmarks. To compensate for this, the authors in [7, 8] defined a *data-driven ranking* solution for each evaluation network dataset. The key idea was to produce a ranking such that a node's score is directly proportional to the nodes' in/out-degree ratio and inversely proportional to the node's influence according to an OSN-specific measure of influence. To this aim, the empirical influence measure defined in [1] was chosen thanks to its simplicity and applicability to any OSN. Originally conceived for Twitter users, this measure estimates the influence of a user based on the amount of tweets that her/his followers have retweeted. This measure was then extended in [7, 8] and adapted to interaction-based networks as well.

© The Author(s), under exclusive license to Springer Nature Switzerland AG 2018   29
A. Tagarelli, R. Interdonato, *Mining Lurkers in Online Social Networks*,
SpringerBriefs in Computer Science, https://doi.org/10.1007/978-3-030-00229-9_4

Results showed that **LurkerRank** achieves high correlation with the data-driven reference ranking and outperforms baselines (i.e., in/out degree distribution) and competing methods like PageRank [5], alpha-centrality [4], and Fair-Bets [6]. In-neighbors-driven and in-out-neighbors-driven **LurkerRank** methods are particularly effective, thus suggesting that in real-world networks principles of *overconsumption* and of *authoritativeness of the information received* tend to be more useful in identifying lurkers than the principle of *non-authoritativeness of the information produced*.

> While exploiting information on the network structure solely, **LurkerRank** methods exhibit the unique ability of detecting non-trivial lurking cases, while conversely existing ranking methods that could be thought of as possible alternatives fail in identifying lurkers.

Other findings from the early studies include aspects related to *reciprocity* and *percolation analysis* Considering the first aspect, it was observed a small or negligible fraction of reciprocal edges between lurkers w.r.t. the total number of edges in the original network graph, as well as a small or negligible fraction of reciprocal edges in the original graph that connect lurkers to each other [8]. Therefore:

> Lurkers are not much prone to reciprocate each other.

Under a percolation analysis framework, it has been shown that lurkers tend to be matched by users that are involved in links with low (directed) topological overlap [8]. As further explored and confirmed in later works (cf. Chap. 7), this would hint that

> A relation exists between lurkers and users playing the role of bridges between communities, under the assumption of lurking-oriented topological graph of an OSN.

Remarkably, the meaningfulness of the ranking solutions produced by **LurkerRank** (as well as produced by selected competing methods) was also assessed through manual inspection of the contents and meta-data available in the public OSN-pages of the top-ranked users. An analysis on Twitter and other OSNs of the available information about the personal profiles and social contacts has revealed that top-ranked users by **LurkerRank** actually have a lurking profile, while conversely competing methods tend to detect users that play other roles in the network.

A further stage of research on the topic was aimed to unveil the behavior of lurkers and their relations with other users over time. The rest of this chapter provides a summary of the research questions addressed and main lessons learned in [9].

4.2   Do Lurkers Match Inactive Users?

Lurking is often related to nonposting behavior. When considering the static picture of a network dataset, one remark that stand out from the analysis in [9] is that the overlap between the set of zero-contributors (i.e., totally inactive users) and the set of potential lurkers (i.e., users with in/out-degree ratio above 1) may vary from 12% on the Flickr favorite-based interaction network to 72 and 95% on the FriendFeed and Instagram comment-based interaction networks, respectively. This would indicate that

> Lurkers are more likely to behave similarly to inactive users when their activity is regarded in terms of time-consuming interactions, such as commenting. By contrast, the overlap between lurkers and inactive users is relatively small when "one-click" interactions (e.g., likes, favorite-markings) are taken into account.

In other terms, the content consumption by lurkers might be driven by the information economy principle of least effort: lurkers tend to exhibit the "like" behavior strikingly more than producing comments, in accord with the intuition that a greater effort (in terms of time and communication economy) must be done to drive the social interaction towards conversation.

4.3   Do Lurkers Match Newcomers?

Lurkers are in principle also related to newcomers, since lurking can depend on a temporary status of learning the etiquette of the community and the proper usage of the services provided by an OSN.

The authors in [9] investigated whether and to what extent lurkers match newcomers during the evolution of a network. In their analysis, a user was regarded as a newcomer at time t if, at any time $t' < t$, s/he was not involved in any interaction with other users. Given a network dataset and relating top-LurkerRank solutions at 5, 10 and 25%, two series over a 6-month timespan were analyzed: the fraction of newcomers that were recognized as lurkers and the fraction of lurkers that were also newcomers.

Considering a like-based interaction scenario, it has been shown that the fraction of lurkers matching newcomers varies from about 30 to 20%, regardless of the selected top-ranked lurkers; by contrast, the fraction of newcomers matching lurkers follows a more constant (and slightly increasing) trend over the timespan, achieving values below 10%, for top-5% and top-10% lurkers, and around 20% for top-25% lurkers. For interactions based on comments, the fraction of newcomers matching lurkers again tends to be roughly constant over time, while the fraction of lurkers matching newcomers can vary significantly depending on the type of OSN (e.g., within 50–20% in FriendFeed, but below 10% on average in Instagram).

Overall, newcomers' behavior can be explained by examining how they tend to be engaged in content production activities by observing their friends' actions. This resembles the Bandura's *observational learning* theory, i.e., learning through being given access to the learning experiences of other users [2]. Therefore, as also confirmed in social science and human-computer interaction research studies:

> Newcomers' behavior, as a form of observational learning, and lurking are related to each other.

4.4 How Frequently Do Lurkers Respond to Others' Actions?

Lurkers can show a limited amount of activity in response to others' contributions to the community life.

Figure 4.1 reports the distributions of time differences (in days) between any two consecutive responsive actions made by a user w.r.t. a post created by her/his followees, over a timespan of 90 days, in Instagram and Flickr. The analysis of such distributions shows how lurkers' responsiveness frequency can be of the order of several days, or weeks, although the latency between any two consecutive responsive actions may significantly vary depending on the network. In fact, to observe 80% of responses, about 18 days would pass in relation to the like-based network of Flickr, but nearly 1 month in the comment-based network of Instagram for the top-25% lurkers (and even longer, i.e., more than 40 days, for the top-5% lurkers). In general,

> The lurkers' responsiveness frequency appears to be twice slower than that exhibited by the users, and this gets larger for more time-consuming responsive actions.

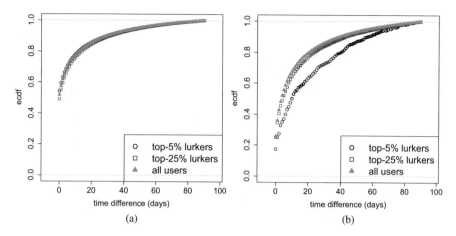

Fig. 4.1 Responsiveness frequency: empirical cumulative distribution function (ecdf) plots of user reaction latency (in days), based on favorites in Flickr (**a**) and comments in Instagram (**b**). (Best viewed in color.) [9]

4.5   Do Lurkers Create Preferential Relations with Active Users?

Another interesting aspect that is studied in [9] corresponds to unveil the dynamics of the binding between lurkers and active users, and how this relates to the popularity of the active users. To this purpose, the authors investigated whether there exist relations between lurkers and active users in terms of *preferential attachment*, that is, whether lurker can link preferentially to active users that already have a large number of connected lurkers, and vice versa. Therefore, based on timestamped followship information in a network, two cases of preferential attachment were considered: new connections received by active users for any k lurkers, and new connections produced by lurkers for any k active users.

To support the above hypothesis in the first case, it was found indeed that

> The number of lurkers shows a good linear correlation with the average number of new links received by active users.

For instance, Fig. 4.2a reports results obtained on Flickr, averaged per user and per week, for each k. In the plot, the least-squared-error linear fit has a slope of 0.00836, which means that on average active users receive per week one new connection from lurkers for every 120 lurker-followers that they already have.

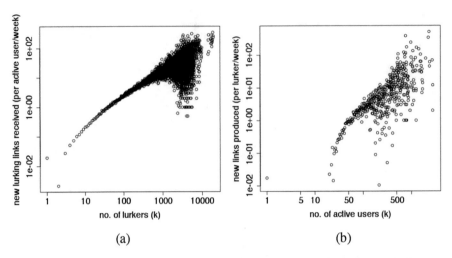

Fig. 4.2 Timestamped followship-based evaluation of preferential attachment between lurkers vs. active users. New connections are detected for each weekly-aggregated network, on Flickr [9]

By contrast, it is unlikely that preferential attachment holds when studying the new connections produced by lurkers for any k active users, as shown in Fig. 4.2b. Therefore,

> Lurkers that have a higher number of active users as followees are not more likely to create new connections to other active users.

4.6 How Do Lurking Trends Evolve?

Further research questions concern how lurking trends change over time, how they can be grouped together, and whether characteristic patterns may arise to indicate different profiles of lurkers.

In order to reveal structures hidden in the lurking trends that vary over time, the users' profiles of lurking scores were modeled as time series and then provided in input to a clustering algorithm [9]. This clustering analysis was conducted by repeatedly applying LurkerRank to successive snapshots of a network. Since the snapshots can vary in size, LurkerRank scores were first normalized to be comparable across different times, before deriving a time series of the normalized LurkerRank scores for every user in the dataset. A *soft clustering* approach, based on the classic fuzzy c-means algorithm, was adopted to group the time series of LurkerRank scores, therefore each time series was assigned with fuzzy memberships to all clusters.

Results corresponded to different scenarios, both in terms of time-granularity (i.e., time series length) and type of relation (i.e., comments, favorite-marks, likes plus comments) underlying the graphs from which the time series were generated. They revealed that

> More time-consuming actions (i.e., comments on Instagram, "likes" plus comments on FriendFeed) tend to correspond to temporal trends that present sharper upward/downward shifts, and to clusters with more noisy data.

Remarkably, from a user engagement perspective, lurking-series do not tend to group into decreasing trends, which would suggest that

> Lurkers are not likely to spontaneously delurk themselves, i.e., to turn their behavior into a more active participation to the community life.

4.7   How Do Topical Interests of Lurkers Evolve?

Adding the content axis to lurking analysis is important to deepen our understanding of the topical usage of lurkers, how lurkers change their topical patterns, and whether these changes might differ from those of the other users. Exploring topic-sensitive evolution patterns of lurking behavior is however difficult, due to limited involvement of lurkers in the production and exchange of content in an OSN.

To answer the above research question, the authors in [9] conduct an experimental evaluation using Instagram data, based on *statistical topic modeling* to learn the topics of interest shown by the users. All media posts of each user were collected as a single document, where the tags assigned by users to their media were selected as document features. Tags occurring in less than five documents or in more than 75% of the documents in the collection were filtered out. The selected tags corresponded to coarse-grain topics, including **nature, travels, photography**-related technical aspects, usage of popular applications for photo/video editing and publishing (e.g., Latergram, VSCO Cam), **attention-seeking** and **microcommunity-focused** tags (e.g., #photooftheday, #igmaster, #justgoshoot, #iphonesia).

Upon the obtained representation, Latent Dirichlet Allocation (LDA) [3] models were learned with 5–50 latent topics, in increments of 5, executing up to 100 iterations; upon a manual inspection of the description of topics learned by the LDA models, the model with 20 topics was finally chosen according to more evidence and richness in terms of both characteristic and discriminating features. This 20-topic LDA model was used to induce topic-sensitive subgraphs from the Instagram user network. To derive each of these subgraphs, the authors first aggregated the finer-grain topics learned by LDA into thematically-cohesive *topic-sets*, then every user was assigned to the topic-set that maximizes the likelihood in the LDA per-document topic distributions.

Using such topic-specific subgraphs, the authors looked for clues about major topics (i.e., frequently used tags) that characterize lurkers. To do this, the top-ranked lurkers detected in the full, topic-independent graph were compared with the top-ranked lurkers detected in each of the topic-specific subgraphs, for a given fraction of top-ranked lurkers (varying at 5, 10 and 25%). Results showed a relatively good matching between the top-ranked lurkers in the full graph and those relating to the subgraph specific of certain topics (e.g., photo art, nature, attention-seeking topics). The above evaluation was also repeated over selected temporal snapshots of the Instagram network, from which it turned out that

> The topic usage behavior of lurkers in each snapshot is mainly characterized by tags that belong to one or more topic-sets.

Moreover, it was observed that, with the exception of the first quarter snapshot, miscellanea tags were rarely chosen by lurkers, thus

> Lurkers are more likely to focus on contents (media) that are well categorized into only one of the identified topic-sets.

In a further stage of analysis concerning the evolution of topical interests over time, the authors hypothesized that lurkers might exhibit patterns of topical interests that do not significantly differ from those of the other (active) users. Figure 4.3 shows two transition diagrams which offer a view of how the topical usage patterns change from one state (i.e., topic-set) to another, over the quarters of year 2013 in Instagram, for all users and for all top-25% lurkers, respectively. Considering first the topical evolution of all users (top of Fig. 4.3), it can be observed that the various levels (i.e., quarters of year 2013) are characterized by a core of topic-sets which, although with varying proportions, are always present over time (i.e., nature, attention-seeking, architecture, and miscellanea). Other topic-sets (e.g., pets and photo art) may correspond to temporary interests of users, as they are present only in some of the levels. Topical usage patterns of the users tend to continuously change over time, which corresponded to transitions from one topic-set state in a level to each of the other states in the next level. This can be explained since users can often adopt tags that naturally belong to more than one topic-set to annotate their media, according to the type of photo or video (e.g., a skyline photo can be equally relevant to the categories photo art, travel, attention-seeking). However, all topic-set states can also show a moderate stability (e.g., second quarter level), that is, a fraction of users could not transition out of a topic-set state once they enter it. Topical usage transitions in the graph of the top-ranked lurkers (bottom of Fig. 4.3) are also highly dynamic. The per-level topic-sets appear to be the same or a subset of those in the all-users graph. This would hence confirm the initial hypothesis that

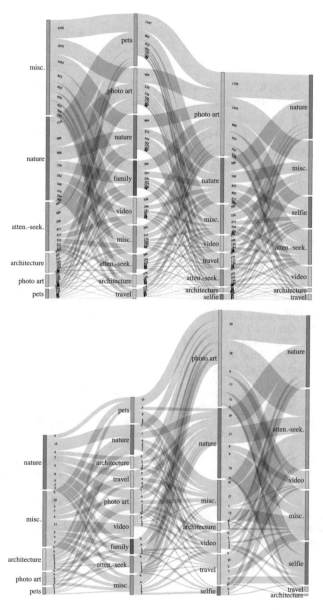

Fig. 4.3 Topic evolution on Instagram: all users (top) vs. top-25% lurkers (bottom). Levels correspond to quarters of year 2013. Each vertical colored box represents a state as an aggregation of topics, which are learned from the network contents at a given time (level). Gray curves correspond to users transitioning from state to state. The portion of each state that does not have outgoing gray lines are users that end in this state. States are labeled with their description and their frequency, i.e., the number of users that are assigned to that topic at that level; gray curves are proportional to the topic level frequencies. (Best viewed in color.) [9]

> Lurkers tend to show patterns of topical interests that do not significantly differ from the ones of all users.

Moreover, in some cases transitions that flow out from a topic-set state are more than the incoming ones, which corresponds to the behavior of lurkers as "newcomers", i.e., lurkers that were not present in the immediately preceding snapshot graph, but could be in earlier snapshots. For instance, while several lurkers showing different interests at the second level end in the photo art state at the third level, a nearly equal proportion of new lurkers start from that state, then transition towards different topic-sets.

References

1. E. Bakshy, J. M. Hofman, W. A. Mason, and D. J. Watts. Everyone's an influencer: quantifying influence on Twitter. In *Proc. ACM Conf. on Web Search and Web Data Mining (WSDM)*, pages 65–74, 2011.
2. A. Bandura. *Social foundations of thought and action: A social cognitive theory*. Englewood Cliffs, NJ: Prentice Hall, 1986.
3. D. M. Blei, A. Y. Ng, and M. I. Jordan. Latent Dirichlet Allocation. *Journal of Machine Learning Research*, 3(4–5):993–1022, 2003.
4. P. Bonacich and P. Lloyd. Eigenvector-like measures of centrality for asymmetric relations. *Social Networks*, 23:191–201, 2001.
5. S. Brin and L. Page. The anatomy of a large-scale hypertextual Web search engine. *Computer Networks and ISDN Systems*, 30(1-7):107–117, 1998.
6. S. Budalakoti and R. Bekkerman. Bimodal invitation-navigation fair bets model for authority identification in a social network. In *Proc. ACM Conf. on World Wide Web (WWW)*, pages 709–718, 2012.
7. A. Tagarelli and R. Interdonato. "Who's out there?": Identifying and Ranking Lurkers in Social Networks. In *Proc. Int. Conf. on Advances in Social Networks Analysis and Mining (ASONAM)*, pages 215–222, 2013.
8. A. Tagarelli and R. Interdonato. Lurking in social networks: topology-based analysis and ranking methods. *Social Netw. Analys. Mining*, 4(230):27, 2014.
9. A. Tagarelli and R. Interdonato. Time-aware analysis and ranking of lurkers in social networks. *Social Netw. Analys. Mining*, 5(1):23, 2015.

Chapter 5
Pervasiveness of the Notion of Lurking in OSNs

Abstract Identifying and mining lurkers finds application in a variety of OSNs other than social media platforms. In this chapter, we put evidence on the pervasiveness of the notion of lurking, utilizing collaboration networks and trust networks as two cases in point. As regards collaboration networks, we focus on a parallel between lurkers and *vicarious learners*, i.e., users who take "non-expert" roles such as apprentices or advisees. We illustrate how to model a *vicarious-learning-oriented* collaboration network and we describe a method to identify and rank vicarious learners on it, namely **VLRank**. The second part of the chapter is devoted to the study of relations between lurkers and trustworthy/untrustworthy users. Through an analysis on who-trusts-whom networks and social media networks, we clarify to what extent the general perception of lurkers as *untrustworthy* users is appropriate or not.

As previously introduced, lurking behaviors build on the participation inequality phenomenon, which characterizes many OSNs. In effect, lurking behaviors hold whenever there is evidence of unbalance between the information consumed with respect to the information produced by users. As a consequence, the problem of identifying and mining lurkers applies not only in social media platforms, but also in many other OSNs.

Consider, for instance, the social networks underlying *peer-to-peer network systems*, such as the popular BitTorrent or Gnutella. Here, lurkers can be studied in the context of analysis of *leeching* behaviors. Leech nodes act like parasites in absorbing others' information without giving anything back, or offering just the bare essential to access the network without being penalized or banned. Specifically, in a peer-to-peer network, a leech is a user downloading a huge amount of data without sharing anything, or disconnecting from the network as soon as s/he completes her/his downloads [5]; however, on some platforms such as BitTorrent, leeching can also be associated to a legitimate practice of incomplete file-sharing. Note that a leeching behavior, despite not being generally illegal, is often considered malicious

© The Author(s), under exclusive license to Springer Nature Switzerland AG 2018

A. Tagarelli, R. Interdonato, *Mining Lurkers in Online Social Networks*,
SpringerBriefs in Computer Science, https://doi.org/10.1007/978-3-030-00229-9_5

or harmful, as it usually violates the community's etiquette. Therefore, it is desirable to identify leeching nodes at various levels in order to design anti-leeching plans in the network (e.g., [9]).

In this chapter we will focus on two different scenarios in order to further demonstrate the pervasiveness of the concept of lurking: research collaboration networks (Sect. 5.1) and online trust contexts (Sect. 5.2).

5.1   Lurking and Collaboration Networks

One scenario where it is possible to observe behaviors analogous to lurking is that occurring in collaboration networks. These can be seen as prototypes of information networks constituted by (possibly) heterogeneous entities (e.g., organizations, people, projects, scientific publications, encyclopedic entries) which interact with each other in order to achieve common or compatible goals. A typical example of collaboration networks is represented by research collaboration networks (RCNs). Here, silent users can be regarded as users who take "non-expert" roles, that is, *apprentices* or *advisees*. Like for online social media networks, such users constitute a significant part of members in the RCN, since an apprenticeship status clearly holds for the initial stage of the researcher lifetime, and also with respect to any topic that at a particular time does not represent the researcher's interests.

A particularly challenging type of relationship to discover from the apprentice perspective concerns *vicarious learning*. While in social learning theory this definition assumes a positive meaning (e.g., people can learn through being given access to the learning experiences of others [4]), in a publication context it can still be identified and measured in collaborations in which one might marginally contribute to the research activity. The problem of identifying and ranking vicarious learners in RCNs is addressed by the authors in [10], who proposed a variant of LurkerRank, called VLRank.

5.1.1   Vicarious-Learning-Oriented RCNs

To model a *vicarious-learning-oriented* RCN, the authors in [10] resemble the lurking-oriented topology (Chap. 3) so that nodes are authors, edges correspond to co-authorship, and the edge orientation is chosen based on the number of publications of each author. More specifically, in the attempt of capturing the knowledge flow from expert to apprentice, each edge is modeled as to start from the co-author with higher number of publications to the co-author with lower number of publications.

The vicarious-learner-oriented RCN graph model is hence defined as a weighted directed graph $\mathscr{G}_t = \langle \mathscr{V}_t, \mathscr{E}_t, w_t \rangle$, where t is a discrete time interval, $\mathscr{V}_t$ is the set of nodes (authors), $\mathscr{E}_t$ is the set of edges, and w_t is an edge weighting function. The semantics of any edge (u, v) is that v is likely most to benefit from the collaboration with u at time t, and the edge weight, $w_t(u, v)$, expresses the strength of the benefit received by v from u. A link $(u, v) \in \mathcal{E}_t$ is drawn from u to v if they are co-authors in some publication at time interval t, with author u having a total number of publications (as calculated at time t or earlier) greater than that of author v; in case of a tie, reciprocal edges are inserted between u and v. Moreover, edges are weighted based on the number of co-authored publications, taking into account a *limited attention* factor, i.e., the strength of an edge (u, v) is weighted not only as directly proportional to the evidence of collaboration in terms of publications but also as inversely proportional to the number of publications co-authored by the advisor u with advisees other than v. Formally, at time t [10]:

$$w_t(u, v) = coPubs(u, v, t) \left(1 - \frac{\sum_{k \in N^{out}(u,t) \setminus \{v\}} coPubs(u, k, t)}{\sum_{k \in N^{out}(u,t)} coPubs(u, k, t)} \right) \quad (5.1)$$

where $coPubs(u, v, t)$ is the number of publications co-authored by u and v at time t, and $N^{out}(u, t)$ denotes the set of u's advisees (i.e., u's out-neighbors) at time t.

5.1.2 The VLRank Method

The **VLRank** method is formulated in [10] as a PageRank-based weighted variant of the **LurkerRank** method based on the in-neighbors-driven lurking model (Chap. 3), that is [10]:

$$VLR(v) = d \left(\frac{1}{|N^{out}(v)|} \sum_{u \in N^{in}(v)} w_t(u, v) \frac{|N^{out}(u)|}{|N^{in}(u)|} \right) VLR(u) + (1 - d)p(v) \quad (5.2)$$

where $w_t(u, v)$ is defined as in Eq. (5.1), $p(v)$ denotes the value for v in the personalization (or teleportation) vector, which is by default set to $1/|\mathcal{V}|$, d is a damping factor ranging within [0,1], usually set to 0.85.

The **VLRank** method was evaluated on a full dump of the *DBLP* computer science bibliography.[1] To study the temporal evolution of the vicarious learners to be identified, subsets corresponding to the last three terms of approximately 3 years were derived to form the vicarious-learning-oriented RCN graph. Effectiveness of **VLRank** was then assessed against two different data-driven rankings, the one based on bibliographic information from DBLP itself, and the other one based on the

---

[1] http://dblp.uni-trier.de/db/.

activity score extracted from the *ArnetMiner* website[2]. Analogously to what the authors did for the **LurkerRank** methods, meaningfulness of **VLRank** was also demonstrated through a qualitative analysis of the top-100 ranked scholars obtained by **VLRank**. Compared to the standard PageRank, **VLRank** has shown to be able to assign highest scores to authors who can be defined vicarious learners with a certain objectivity, while the top-ranked list by PageRank contained authors who were more likely to be defined as team leaders or, at least, active contributors. **VLRank** has also shown to be more effective than PageRank in capturing the temporal evolution of vicarious learners, as demonstrated by the results of the experiments on the 3-year subsets of DBLP [10].

5.2 Lurking and Trust Contexts

Active users tend to avoid wasting their time with people who are very likely to not reply or show slow responsiveness, or who have few/bad feedbacks. As a consequence, the above remark would lead us to think that:

> Lurkers could in principle be perceived as *untrustworthy* users.

Within this view, a challenge is hence to model the dynamics of lurking behaviors in trust contexts [1], and ultimately unveil relations between lurkers and trustworthy/untrustworthy users in ranking problems. In the following, we discuss some research works that go in the above outlined direction.

5.2.1 *TrustRank-Biased LurkerRank*

The study in [11] provides a preliminary insight into a comparison of **LurkerRank** methods with a state-of-the-art method for ranking pages/users according to their trustworthiness, namely *TrustRank* [6].

The TrustRank algorithm is substantially a biased PageRank in which the personalization set corresponds to the "good part" of an a-priori selected seed set. The seed set is chosen to be comprised of a relatively small subset of nodes in the graph, each of which is labeled as either trustworthy or untrustworthy by some *oracle* function. The ability of detecting trustworthy users featured by TrustRank is integrated into **LurkerRank** in order to improve the *trustworthiness* of the lurkers to be detected. In the resulting set of methods, named **TrustRank-biased LurkerRank**, the uniform

---

[2]http://arnetminer.org/AcademicStatistics.

personalization vector of a **LurkerRank** method is replaced by the ranking vector produced by TrustRank over the same network.

Since, differently from trust network data, OSNs do not contain explicit trust assessments among users, the authors in [11] choose to infer behavioral trust information from an OSN based on user interactions that would provide an intuitive way of indicating trust in another user, as also suggested in prior research (e.g., [2]). Focusing on the case of the well-known photo sharing platform *Flickr*, the authors leverage information on the number of favorite markings received by a user's photographs as implicit trust statements. In order to define the oracle function based on the above indicators of trust, they postulate that the higher the number of users that indicate trust in a user u, the more likely is the trustworthiness of u. They then formalize this intuition as an entropy-based oracle function H, in such a way that for any user u [11]:

$$H(u) = -\frac{1}{\log |N(u)|} \sum_{v \in N(u)} \frac{ET(v,u)}{\sum_{k \in N(u)} ET(k,u)} \log \left(\frac{ET(v,u)}{\sum_{k \in N(u)} ET(k,u)} \right) \tag{5.3}$$

where $N(u)$ is the set of neighbors of node u, and $ET(v,u)$ is the empirical trust function measuring the number of implicit trust statements (i.e., favorites) assigned by node v to node u. A user u will be regarded as "good" if the corresponding $H(u)$ belongs to the third quartile of the distribution of H values over all users.

Experimental results showed that all **LurkerRank** methods are positively correlated with TrustRank, thus indicating that the trustworthiness of users is likely to be considered when ranking lurkers. By personalizing a **LurkerRank** method with TrustRank, the correlation with TrustRank itself generally increases, while all **TrustRank-biased LurkerRank** methods still show a strong correlation with their respective original **LurkerRank** method. Summing up, this suggests that introducing a trust-oriented bias in **LurkerRank** methods would not significantly decrease their lurker ranking effectiveness, while also accounting for the user trustworthiness.

5.2.2 Lurking and Trustworthiness in Ranking Problems

A further advance in research on relations between lurking behavior and trust contexts is presented in [7], focusing on the investigation of how and to what extent lurkers are related to trustworthy and untrustworthy users. In that study, trust and distrust notions are regarded in terms of two different scenarios. The first scenario is the classic one in trust computing, which concerns *who-trusts-whom* networks (e.g., Advogato, Epinions) where explicit trust statements are available for every pair of users, therefore an analogy was considered between lurkers and users that take the role of "observer", or at most "apprentice". The second scenario refers instead to social media networks, in which trust statements are not directly available, hence they need to be inferred from user interactions (i.e., based on implicit trust statements, as done in [11]).

The entropy-based oracle function reported in Eq. (5.3) is used to infer the likelihood of a user to be trustworthy, thus enabling the use of TrustRank and its counterpart called *Anti-TrustRank* [8], an algorithm similar to Trust-Rank but designed to detect untrustworthy pages.

The analysis conducted in [7] is structured in two main evaluation steps. The first evaluation step is based on trust and distrust evaluation, focusing on the Advogato and Epinions networks, which provide explicit trust indicators that can be regarded as a ground-truth. Results indicate that, as expected, TrustRank performs generally better than **LurkerRank** when detecting trustworthy users, even though the out-neighbors-driven **LurkerRank** methods (Chap. 3) show comparably, and in some case, better performances than TrustRank on the Epinions network. As regards the evaluation of untrustworthy users, performance of Anti-TrustRank and in-out-neighbors-driven **LurkerRank** turn out to be very close. The second evaluation step focuses on rank correlation analysis. Both in trust networks and OSNs, out-neighbors-driven **LurkerRank** methods show higher correlation with TrustRank than the other **LurkerRank** formulations.

Summarizing, the results obtained in [7] on Advogato, Epinions, Flickr and FriendFeed networks have provided the following two useful indications:

> Lurkers should not be a-priori flagged as untrustworthy users.

> Trustworthy users can indeed be found among lurkers.

5.2.3   Lurking and Data Privacy Preservation

In [3], the problem of lurker detection is addressed in a data privacy preservation context, i.e., under the hypothesis that users in an OSN may want to remove their friendship with possible lurkers in order to preserve their data privacy. For this purpose, the authors propose a heterogeneous social network (HSN) model based on hypergraphs, in order to take into account the different types of relations and interactions that can happen on a social media platform.

An HSN is defined as a tuple $(\mathcal{V}, \mathcal{E}, I, \omega)$, where $\mathcal{V}$ is a finite set of vertices, $\mathcal{E}$ is a hyperedges with a finite set of indexes I, and $\omega : \mathcal{E} \rightarrow [0, 1]$ is a weighting function. The set of vertices is in turn defined as $\mathcal{V} = U \cup O \cup T$, where U is a set of users (i.e., the set of persons and organization constituting a social community), O a set of objects (i.e., the user-generated items that are of interest within a given social community) and T a set of topics (i.e., the most significant terms or named entities exploited by users to describe items). Moreover, a *social path* in the HSN is a sequence of distinct vertices and hyperedges that can connect two nodes by leveraging different kinds of relationships; for instance, a path can directly connect two users because they are friends or members of the same group, or indirectly, as they have shared the same picture or commented the same video.

After adapting major centrality measures for their HSN model (i.e., degree, closeness, betweenness centrality), the authors introduce a *neighborhood centrality* measure that expresses the number of nodes that are reachable within a certain number of steps using social paths. The neighborhood centrality relies on the concept of λ-nearest neighbors set. Given a vertex $v \in \mathcal{V}$ of an HSN, the λ-nearest neighbor set of v is the subset of vertices NN_v^λ such that, $\forall u \in NN_v^\lambda$, it holds $d_{min}(v, u) \leq \lambda$ with $u \in U$, where $d_{min}(v, u)$ is the length of the shortest hyperpath between the two vertices.

Given a threshold λ, the neighborhood centrality of a vertex $v \in \mathcal{V}$ of an HSN is then defined as [3]:

$$nc(v) = \frac{|NN_v^\lambda| \cap \mathcal{V}}{|\mathcal{V}| - 1}. \tag{5.4}$$

The authors propose a heuristic algorithm based on the hypothesis that lurkers can be regarded as nodes showing low neighborhood centrality that are connected to nodes having higher neighborhood centrality. Experimental evaluation was performed on the popular Yelp website, using a data-driven ranking based on empirical influence (the same as described in Chap. 4), showing effectiveness in the identification of lurkers under the proposed HSN context.

References

1. S. Adali. *Modeling Trust Context in Networks*. Springer Briefs in Computer Science. Springer, 2013.
2. Sibel Adali, Robert Escriva, Mark K. Goldberg, Mykola Hayvanovych, Malik Magdon-Ismail, Boleslaw K. Szymanski, William A. Wallace, and Gregory Todd Williams. Measuring behavioral trust in social networks. In *Proc. IEEE Int. Conf. on Intelligence and Security Informatics, ISI*, pages 150–152, 2010.
3. Flora Amato, Vincenzo Moscato, Antonio Picariello, Francesco Piccialli, and Giancarlo Sperlì. Centrality in heterogeneous social networks for lurkers detection: An approach based on hypergraphs. *Concurrency and Computation: Practice and Experience*, 30(3), 2018.
4. A. Bandura. *Social foundations of thought and action: A social cognitive theory*. Englewood Cliffs, NJ: Prentice Hall, 1986.
5. P. Dhungel, D. Wu, B. Schonhorst, and K. W. Ross. A measurement study of attacks on BitTorrent leechers. In *Proc. Conf. on Peer-to-peer systems (IPTPS)*, page 7, 2008.
6. Z. Gyöngyi, H. Garcia-Molina, and J. O. Pedersen. Combating Web Spam with TrustRank. In *Proc. Int. Conf. on Very Large Data Bases (VLDB)*, pages 576–587, 2004.
7. R. Interdonato and A. Tagarelli. To trust or not to trust lurkers?: Evaluation of lurking and trustworthiness in ranking problems. In *Proc. Int. School and Conf. on Network Science (NetSciX)*, 2016.

8. V. Krishnan and R. Raj. Web Spam Detection with Anti-Trust Rank. In *Proc. Int. Workshop on Adversarial Information Retrieval on the Web (AIRWeb)*, pages 37–40, 2006.

9. X. Meng and J. Jin. A free rider aware topological construction strategy for search in unstructured p2p networks. *Peer-to-Peer Netw. Appl.*, 9:127–141, 2016.

10. A. Tagarelli and R. Interdonato. Ranking Vicarious Learners in Research Collaboration Networks. In *Proc. 15th Int. Conf. on Asia-Pacific Digital Libraries (ICADL)*, pages 93–102, 2013.

11. A. Tagarelli and R. Interdonato. Lurking in social networks: topology-based analysis and ranking methods. *Social Netw. Analys. Mining*, 4(230):27, 2014.

Chapter 6
Delurking

Abstract Encouraging lurkers to more actively participate in the OSN life, a.k.a. delurking, is desirable in order to make lurkers' social capital available to other users. In this chapter, we discuss in detail the delurking problem and computational approaches to solve it. We first provide an overview of works focusing on user engagement methodologies to understand how users can be motivated to participate and contribute to the community living in a social environment. Then we concentrate on the presentation of algorithmic solutions to support the task of persuading lurkers to become active participants in their OSN.

It might be desirable that lurkers, or a portion of them, are nurtured and eventually persuaded to be more actively engaged in the OSN community by other users which, intuitively, may take on different roles, including influencers, elders, masters. However, as discussed in Sect. 2.4, "delurking the lurkers" is challenging: in fact, most of the existing studies addressing this problem have focused on the conceptualization of main strategies for delurking, from a social science and human-computer interaction perspective. Given the variety and complexity of the influencing factors that drive online participation (cf. Sect. 2.3), developing a computational approach to turn lurkers into active members of an OSN appears to be difficult, regardless of the delurking strategy adopted.

6.1 User Engagement in Online Social Networks

User engagement concerns methodologies to understand how users can be motivated to participate and contribute to the community living in a social environment. In the context of OSNs, determining and predicting user engagement is crucial not only to support the analysis of online user behaviors, but also to solve several practical tasks such as design of social media platforms, service personalization, targeted advertising, and many more.

47

While the general concept of user engagement can be considered intuitive, several formal definitions exist in the literature. User engagement has been traditionally defined as a category of user experience, or as a form of involvement (i.e., engaging) and participation (i.e., the act of being engaged), thus suggesting engagement be both a psychological state and a behavior [11]. Ray et al. [37] define engagement as "a holistic psychological state in which one is cognitively and emotionally energized to socially behave in ways that exemplify the positive ways in which group members prefer to think of themselves". Di Gangi et al. [11] observe that previous definitions of user engagement do not clarify to what extent it is part of user experience, of user behavior, and/or a psychological state. They then define user engagement as the psychological state resulting from user experience, which is in turn composed of social interactions and the technical features of a social media platform. Under this view, user engagement is seen as a mental state that influences user's behavior.

Research on user engagement has often focused on analyzing the causes of different types of engagement on specific platforms or during specific usage scenarios. In [24] a survey-based analysis is conducted on the engagement of YouTube users, with the goal of detecting the main causes (i.e., motivating factors) of different participatory and consumption behaviors. The authors find that the main motivating factors that lead to commenting and uploading behaviors are those related to social interactions, while sharing actions are strongly related to information giving factors. Conversely, liking and disliking actions seem to be related to nearly all the factors taken into account, with a slightest predominance of personal entertainment factors. Hodas et al. [17] study social media usage during disaster scenarios, combining information from electroencephalograms (EEGs), personality surveys, and inclination to share social media. Results indicate that extroverts are more likely to share content, but also that individuals with depressive personalities are the most likely cohort to share informative content, like news or alerts.

Given the difficulty in formulating an exact and comprehensive definition, and in identifying all the influence sources, measuring and predicting user engagement is a challenging task per se. In [34] a specific questionnaire, namely the User Engagement Scale (UES), is proposed as a robust measure of user engagement. Results on three empirical studies in the online news domain indicate that aesthetics, usability, and focused attention appear to be stable dimensions of an engaged experience across various types of digital media, whereas felt involvement, novelty, and endurability are more variable in terms of whether they are stand-alone factors. OSN-specific features have also been used to predict user engagement. In [30] a study is conducted on organizational Facebook pages, where user engagement is predicted based on likes, comments and shares, response time and rate of comments. This analysis shows how predicting user engagement in OSN is a highly complex scenario, where it is hardly possible to find general tendencies—the impact of features on user engagement highly depends on the specific characteristics of each organization. However, the authors also identify some general trend, such as the clear overall positive correlations between likes and comments, or between likes and shares, and the fact that engagement with a post can be predicted based on activity levels in the first hour after it is posted. A similar approach is used in [25], where a data mining framework is proposed for the segmentation of users in an OSN based on their engagement level, namely apathetic, staunch, ordinary and lazy users, using as features likes, comments, and post polarity. Rossetti et al. [39] observe that the tendency in addressing the user engagement problem at the single individual level may be ineffective in most cases, since there may be a consistent redundancy given that neighbors in networks tend to behave in a similar way showing a certain degree of homophily. Starting from this observation the authors address user engagement analysis at the level of groups of users (social communities), focusing on the Skype social network, finding that user engagement can be successfully predicted based on topological and geographic features of social communities. In [18], degree and presence of user engagement on Twitter are measured. The presence of a user's Twitter engagement with respect to a specific event is defined as the existence of at least one tweet (or retweet or mention) that references that event. The degree of a user's Twitter engagement is measured by the number of tweets that they post regarding that event (i.e., the more the tweets, the higher the engagement with the event). The authors conduct a statistical study about the variables that influence these engagement factors, such as Twitter activities (prior to the user engagement with an event), tweets' content (including topical interests), geolocation (the user's geographical proximity to the event), and social network structure (the followers, followees and common neighbors of the user). They find that although each of the variables can have an impact on user engagement depending on the specific event, user's prior activities and social network structure appear to be the best predictors of user engagement for both presence and degree aspects. Studies regarding the prediction of user engagement have also been performed in the domain of intelligent assistants [41], native advertisements [5], and brand loyalty [52].

Delurking as a Form of User Engagement. The act of *delurking* can easily be seen as a form of user engagement. Ad-hoc techniques and strategies have been proposed to enhance user engagement in specific contexts, such as gamification strategies [9], and strategies based on the support and guidance from elder, active members of the community (possibly, experts, opinion leaders, etc.) [27, 44]. In a study by Nazi et al. [31], the delurking problem is addressed by focusing on an automatic way to simplify the reviewing task of web items of interest, thus engaging lurkers in commenting activities. The motivation for this study stems from the fact that writing a detailed review for a product or service is usually time-consuming and may not offer an incentive. Therefore, through a recommendation approach, a lurker would quickly choose from among the set of recommended tags to articulate her/his feedback for the item without having to spend a lot of time writing the review.

6.2 Self-Delurking Randomization

The authors in [45] define a "self-delurking" randomization model, named *delurking-oriented randomization*, to simulate a mechanism of disclosure of the presence of lurkers, i.e., to simulate introducing of selected lurkers to active users.

Randomized models are commonly used to monitor how varying a certain topological feature may impact on the dynamics of the network. The most widely applied randomized model uses the concept of *rewiring*, so that the edges of the original (undirected) network are randomly rewired pairwise.

The key idea behind the method proposed in [45] is to exploit the rewiring mechanism in order to induce more-likely-active users virtually hear from less-likely-active users. The method, whose pseudo-code is sketched in Algorithm 1, works by inserting new connections into the network each of which randomly links a vertex selected from the top of a predetermined LurkerRank solution to a vertex selected from the bottom of that ranking. The algorithm hence requires cut-off thresholds to control the selection of the head and tail of the LurkerRank distribution, and a percentage threshold to control the degree of delurking-oriented randomization (i.e., the fraction of potentially new edges to add to the graph). At each step of insertion of a new pair of edges, it is to be ensured that both the new formed edges do not already exist in the graph. This restriction prevents the appearance of multiple edges connecting the same pair of vertices. Note that the algorithm does not provide a proper randomization model in its usual definition, since both the size of the network and the degree of vertices will change.

A major goal of the evaluation of the algorithm was to analyze the correlation of the LurkerRank solution before and after the randomization. Using rewiring probability of 0.5, cut-off thresholds at 25%, and by varying the degree of randomization within [0.1, 1.0], it turned out that the correlation is mostly low, when sink and source nodes are discarded. In general, the top-ranked lurkers may significantly change w.r.t. the original topology of the network, also for different

---

Algorithm 1 Delurking-Oriented Randomization [45]

Input: The topology graph $\mathscr{G} = \langle \mathscr{V}, \mathscr{E} \rangle$ of an OSN. The ranking L corresponding to a LR solution
　　for $\mathscr{G}$. Cut-off percentage thresholds t_1, t_2 of ranking order in L. Probability p. Maximum
　　fraction d of new edges to add to $\mathscr{G}$.
Output: A randomized graph $\mathscr{G}'$.
　1: $\mathscr{E}' \leftarrow \emptyset$
　2: Sort L by decreasing lurking score
　3: Let L_{top} (resp. L_{bottom}) be the top-t_1 (resp. bottom-t_2) of the sorted L
　4: $E_{al} \leftarrow \{e = (a, l) \in \mathscr{E} \mid a \in L_{\text{bottom}}, l \in L_{\text{top}}\}$
　5: **repeat**
　6:　　Pick randomly with probability p an edge $(a_1, l_1) \in E_{al} \setminus \mathscr{E}'$
　7:　　Pick randomly with probability p an edge $(a_2, l_2) \in E_{al} \setminus \mathscr{E}'$, with $a_2 \neq a_1, l_2 \neq l_1$
　8:　　　$\mathscr{E}' \leftarrow \mathscr{E}' \cup \{(l_1, a_2), (l_2, a_1)\}$　　　　　　　　　　　　/* add new edges */
　9: **until** $(|\mathscr{E}'| \geq d|E_{al}|)$
　10: $\mathscr{G}' \leftarrow \langle \mathscr{V}, \mathscr{E} \cup \mathscr{E}' \rangle$

degrees of randomization. Nonetheless, such an alteration of the topology through the insertion of new links, actually do not significantly change the topological features based on in- and out-degree distributions, since the correlation between the in/out ranking in the original network and each of the in/out rankings of the randomized networks revealed to be moderate to high.

6.3 Delurking and Influence Propagation

The authors in [20, 22] concentrate on the definition of a computational approach to turn lurkers into active participants in the social network. They originally address the problem under the framework of *influence propagation and maximization*. The key intuition is that, if the influence to be propagated in a social network is shaped so to correspond to the effect of any well-established delurking action, then influential users in the network can reach some of the lurkers and persuade them to become more active participants in the social network.

Before getting into the details of the approach proposed in [20, 22], we first provide basics on information diffusion modeling and related influence propagation and maximization problems.

6.3.1 *Information Diffusion and Influence Maximization*

Identifying influential users in an OSN is one of the fundamental problems, also from a marketing viewpoint. Indeed, the idea behind the so-called *viral marketing* is that by identifying the most influential users in the network, a chain reaction of influence can be activated and driven by word-of-mouth, in such a way that with a small marketing cost a large portion of the network can be reached; in other words, if one convinces other users to adopt a product (e.g., by offering discounts or free samples), then these users will endorse the product among their friends, and this will lead to a large number of adoptions, driven by word-of-mouth effect. Such a concept of viral marketing can easily be extended to any intangible item, including information messages, and therefore is also valuable for social network analysis and mining tasks.

Therefore, the viral marketing problem is typically formulated as an optimization problem, in which the objective is, given a budget k that corresponds to the initial marketing investment, to find a set of k users that can maximize the spread of influence through the network, that is, to find the best k users to influence the maximum number of users through the network. Such k users to be identified are called early-adopters or initial influencers, since they represent the seeds for the influence propagation process. This optimization problem is generally referred to as *influence maximization* (e.g., [6, 12, 23, 28, 48]); moreover, when the influence is directed towards a specific audience (i.e., a subset of nodes in the network), the problem is often referred to as *targeted influence maximization* [14, 15, 46, 51].

The spread of influence is subject to rules defined according to a selected *information diffusion* model. The generally adopted operational view of an information diffusion model is that the diffusion process unfolds in discrete time steps in a directed graph, where nodes are users and each edge is associated with a weight expressing the diffusion probability or influence degree from one node to another—intuitively, the activation of a node means that a user is influenced by other users so to "become aware of" or "adopt" a piece of information—and the following rules hold: nodes start either active or inactive, an active may trigger activation of neighboring nodes, active nodes never deactivate (i.e., node can switch to active from inactive status, but the opposite does not hold). Moreover, given a set S of active nodes selected to start the diffusion, the influence spread of S is the expected number of activated nodes at the end of the diffusion process.

Research on information diffusion in OSNs (e.g., [2, 3, 13, 40, 50]) is well-established due to a plethora of methods that have been developed in the last years, mostly upon the two seminal models, namely *Independent Cascade* (IC) and *Linear Threshold* (LT) [23, 49]. Under the IC model, given an initial set of active nodes, the diffusion process unfolds in discrete steps according to the following randomized rules. For any node u that is active at time t, it is given a single chance to activate each currently inactive out-neighbor v; it succeeds with a probability p_{uv}—a parameter of the model—independently of the previous activations. If v has multiple newly activated in-neighbors, their attempts are sequenced in an arbitrary order. If u succeeds, then v will become active in step $t + 1$; but whether or not u succeeds, it cannot make any further attempts to activate v in subsequent rounds. The process terminates when no more activations are possible. The LT model mainly differs from the IC one since exposure to multiple sources of influence is needed for a user before taking a decision. Accordingly, in addition to the influence probabilities on the edges, nodes are assigned with values (randomly drawn from a uniform distribution in [0,1]), which are regarded as node activation thresholds: for any node v that is inactive at time t, if the sum of the influence weights of active in-neighbors of u is above the activation threshold of u then u will be active in step $t + 1$.

Influence maximization under both IC and LT models is NP-hard. There are two sources of complexity: (i) modeling the influence diffusion process and computing the expected number of active nodes, given a seed set of initial influencers, and (ii) discovering the best k spreaders, i.e., the nodes that can maximize the spread under a given diffusion model. Nonetheless, one good news is that an approximate solution can be designed with theoretical guarantee, provided that the natural diminishing property holds for the considered problem. More specifically, it has been shown that for some diffusion models, including IC and LT, the function mapping any subset of nodes to the size of the final active set satisfies monotonicity and submodularity by exploiting the *equivalent live-edge graph model* [23]. This result ensures that a greedy algorithm approximates the optimum within a factor of $(1 - 1/e)$, that is, the discovered seed set activates at least $(1 - 1/e)$ (i.e., 63%) of the number of nodes that the optimal size-k set could activate.

6.3.2 Delurking-Oriented Targeted Influence Maximization

The main contribution in [20] is the definition of an instance of targeted influence maximization in which lurkers are regarded as the target of the diffusion process. A key aspect is that the outcome of a diffusion process has an intuitive analogy in the lurking analysis setting under consideration: the information to spread corresponds to the effect of a delurking strategy, the lurking score associated to each user is related to the effort needed to delurk that user, and his/her activation would hence represent the gain deriving from delurking that user. Moreover, the probabilistic nature of the information diffusion process lends itself particularly well to express a complex behavioral problem like delurking, where the outcome in terms of user engagement is intrinsically uncertain. In this regard, the LT model appears to be more realistic than the IC model, since its ability of reflecting the cumulative effect of exposure to multiple sources of influence, can be profitably exploited to maximize the likelihood of turning a lurker into a user with a more active participation role in the OSN.

Following the notations in [20], let $\mathcal{G}_0 = \langle \mathcal{V}, \mathcal{E} \rangle$ denote a directed graph representing an OSN, with set of nodes $\mathcal{V}$ and set of edges $\mathcal{E}$. Upon $\mathcal{G}_0$, the directed weighted graph $\mathcal{G} = \mathcal{G}_0(b, \ell) = \langle \mathcal{V}, \mathcal{E}, b, \ell \rangle$ is defined to represent the information diffusion graph associated with $\mathcal{G}_0$, where $b : \mathcal{E} \rightarrow \mathbb{R}^*$ is an edge weighting function, and $\ell : \mathcal{V} \rightarrow \mathbb{R}^*$ is a node weighting function.

The latter two functions are assumed to be completely specified based upon the availability of a method able to assign every user with a score that expresses the status of lurking behavior taken by that user (cf. Chap. 3). In this way, for any edge (u, v) in $\mathcal{G}$, the weight $b(u, v)$ indicates the degree of contribution of u to the v's lurking score calculated by the lurker ranking method, which resembles a measure of "influence" exerted by u towards v. Also, the node weight $\ell(v)$ indicates the status of v as lurker, such as higher values of the lurker ranking score of v will correspond to higher $\ell(v)$. More in detail, the node weighting function $\ell(\cdot)$ is defined upon scaling and normalizing the stationary distribution produced by the **LurkerRank** algorithm over $\mathcal{G}_0$. For each node $v \in \mathcal{V}$, the *node lurking value* $\ell(v) \in [0, 1)$ is defined as [20]:

$$\ell(v) = \frac{\tilde{\pi}_v - min_r}{(max_r - min_r) + \epsilon_r}, \tag{6.1}$$

where $\tilde{\pi}$ denotes the stationary distribution of the lurker ranking scores (π) divided by the base-10 power of the order of magnitude of the minimum value in π, $\tilde{\pi}_v$ is the value of $\tilde{\pi}$ corresponding to node v, $max_r = \max_{u \in \mathcal{V}} \tilde{\pi}_u$, $min_r = \min_{u \in \mathcal{V}} \tilde{\pi}_u$, and ϵ_r is a smoothing constant proportional to the order of magnitude of the max_r

value. Information derived from the ranking solution obtained by LurkerRank is also exploited to compute the edge weights, so that for every edge $(u, v) \in \mathcal{E}$ the weight is proportional to the fraction of the original lurking score of v given by its in-neighbor u [20]:

$$b(u, v) = e^{\ell(v)-1} \left[\sum_{w \in N^{in}(v)} \frac{out(w)}{in(w)} \pi_w \right]^{-1} \frac{out(u)}{in(u)} \pi_u, \tag{6.2}$$

where the exponential term is introduced in such a way that the weight on (u, v) will be subject to exponential smoothing for higher $\ell(v)$, in order to require more active in-neighbors to activate a user with higher lurking score. Note also that the above equation meets the LT-based requirement that the sum of incoming edge weights is superiorly bounded by 1.

Upon the above presented diffusion graph model, the authors in [20] define the *DElurking-Oriented Targeted Influence maximizatiON* (DEvOTION) problem, whose objective function is defined in terms of the cumulative amount of lurking scores associated with the nodes in the final active set. This quantity is called *delurking capital*. Formally, given $\mathcal{G} = \langle \mathcal{V}, \mathcal{E}, b, \ell \rangle$, a diffusion model on $\mathcal{G}$, a budget k, and a minimum lurking-score threshold $LS \in [0, 1]$, the DEvOTION objective is to find a seed set $S \subseteq \mathcal{V}$ with $|S| \leq k$ of nodes such that, by activating them, the final active set $\mu(S) \subseteq \mathcal{V}$ will have the maximum delurking capital [20]:

$$S = \underset{S' \subseteq \mathcal{V} \ s.t. \ |S'| \leq k}{\operatorname{argmax}} DC(\mu(S')), \tag{6.3}$$

where $DC(\mu(S))$ is the delurking capital associated with $\mu(S)$:

$$DC(\mu(S)) = \sum_{\substack{v \in \mu(S) \setminus S \ \wedge \\ \ell(v) \geq LS}} \ell(v). \tag{6.4}$$

A major difference of the objective function of the DEvOTION problem w.r.t. the one defined for LT and IC models is that, instead of the expected spread (i.e., the size of the final active set $|\mu(S)|$), it considers the cumulative amount of the scores associated with the activated (target) nodes, i.e., $DC(\mu(S))$. On the other hand, one common aspect with classic IM problems is that the DEvOTION problem is computationally intractable. In this regard, the authors proved that the objective function of DEvOTION satisfies the properties of monotonicity and submodularity under the LT model, that is, function $DC(\mu(A))$ mapping each active set $\mu(A) \subseteq \mathcal{V}$ to its overall delurking capital, is monotone and submodular, for any $LS \in [0, 1]$ [20]. Therefore, the typical $1 - 1/e - \epsilon$ approximation ratio holds for any greedy method to be designed for discovering a k-node set that maximizes the delurking capital in the network for a given threshold LS.

Algorithm 2 The DElurking Oriented Targeted Influence maximizatiON (DEvOTION) Algorithm [20]

Input: A graph $\mathscr{G} = \langle \mathscr{V}, \mathscr{E}, b, \ell \rangle$, a budget (seed set size) k, a lurking threshold $LS \in [0, 1]$, a path pruning threshold $\eta \in [0, 1]$.
Output: Seed set S.

```
 1: S ← ∅
 2: T ← 𝒱                              {nodes that can reach target nodes}
 3: TargetSet ← ∅                      {stores the target nodes at current iteration}
 4: for u ∈ 𝒱 do
 5:     if ℓ(u) ≥ LS then
 6:         TargetSet ← TargetSet ∪ {u}
 7:     end if
 8: end for
 9: while |S| < k do
10:     bestSeed, bestSeed.DC ← −1    {keeps track of the node with the highest spread}
11:     for u ∈ T \ S do
12:         u.DC ← 0                   {initializes each node's spread to zero}
13:     end for
14:     T ← ∅;
15:     for u ∈ TargetSet \ S do
16:         backward(⟨u⟩, 1, ℓ(u))
17:     end for
18:     if bestSeed ≠ −1 then
19:         S ← S ∪ {bestSeed}
20:     else
21:         break
22:     end if
23: end while
24: return S

25: procedure backward(𝒫, pp, score)
26:     u ← 𝒫.last()
27:     T ← T ∪ {u}
28:     while v ∈ Nⁱⁿ(u) ∧ v ∉ S ∪ 𝒫.nodeSet() do
29:         pp ← pp × b(v, u)         {updates the path probability}
30:         if pp ≥ η then
31:             v.DC ← v.DC + pp × score
32:             if v.DC > bestSeed.DC then
33:                 bestSeed ← v       {sets the best seed node as v}
34:             end if
35:             backward(𝒫.append(v), pp, score)
36:         end if
37:     end while
```

A sketch of the pseudocode of the greedy algorithm for **DEvOTION** is shown in Algorithm 2 [20]. The parameter η is introduced for computational efficiency reason, since it controls the size of the neighborhood within which paths are enumerated, under the assumption that the majority of influence can be captured by exploring the paths within a relatively small neighborhood [12]; this means that, for higher η values, fewer paths will be explored (i.e., paths will be pruned earlier).

The algorithm performs a backward visit of $\mathcal{G}$ starting from the nodes identified as target, i.e., the nodes u with $\ell(u) \geq LS$. Moving backward from the target nodes allows the algorithm to ignore all the paths starting from nodes that cannot reach any target, which means reducing its running time without affecting its accuracy. Looking at the algorithmic scheme, all nodes are initially examined to identify the target ones ($TargetSet$) (Lines 4–8). For each iteration of the main loop (Lines 9–19), DEvOTION computes the set T of nodes that reach the target ones and keeps track, into the variable $bestSeed$, of the node with the highest marginal gain (i.e., delurking capital DC). Set T is found at the end of each iteration upon calling the subroutine backward over all nodes in $TargetSet$ that do not belong to the current seed set S (Lines 15–17). This subroutine takes a path $\mathcal{P}$, its probability pp, and the lurking score of the end node in the path (i.e., a target node), and extends $\mathcal{P}$ as much as possible (i.e., as long as pp is not lower than η). Initially (Line 16), a path is formed by one target node, with probability 1. Then (Lines 28–37), the path is extended by exploring the graph backward, adding to it one, unexplored in-neighbor v at time, in a depth-first fashion. The path probability is updated (Line 29) according to the LT-equivalent "live-edge" model, and so the delurking capital (Line 31). The process terminates when no more nodes can be added to the path.

The DEvOTION method was evaluated over OSN datasets of different characteristics and sizes (Instagram, Google+, FriendFeed), in order to assess [20, 22]: performance in terms of estimation of the delurking capital and distribution of target nodes in the final active set, sensitivity to the various parameters, relevance and effectiveness through a comparative analysis with respect to baseline methods and state-of-the-art targeted and non-targeted IM methods, including SimPath [12], TIM+ [48], and KB-TIM [29]. Remarkably, regarding the comparison of DEvOTION with other LT-based IM algorithms, DEvOTION has always shown higher performance in terms of delurking capital, thus providing an unprecedented and appropriate solution for delurking tasks in OSNs.

6.3.3   Community-Based Delurking

The previously described approach allows for discovering a set of active users in an OSN that are likely to influence/engage selected lurkers. One interesting aspect of study in this context is whether and to what extent lurkers and their potential influencers are found to be located in strategical parts of the network.

In [21], the authors address the above aspect by turning it into the following questions:

- How the initial influencers to be learned change by varying the constraints on the portion of information diffusion graph used to reach the target nodes?
- Given an available organization of the network into densely connected substructures as communities, are the target lurkers activated from influencers that belong to the same community, or to external communities?

To answer the above questions, the authors first concentrate on how to constrain the target-specific diffusion graph according to an available community structure, which can be predetermined by any community detection algorithm [32, 47]. They define alternative schemes that differ in the way the community containing a target lurker is expanded and used as the context diffusion graph. Given a diffusion graph $\mathcal{G} = \langle \mathcal{V}, \mathcal{E}, b, \ell \rangle$ and a community structure $\mathcal{C} = \{\mathcal{G}_1, \ldots, \mathcal{G}_H\}$ over $\mathcal{G}$, an *expansion* of a given community $\mathcal{G}_h \in \mathcal{C}$ is a subgraph formed by the union of $\mathcal{G}_h$ with one or more subgraphs in $\mathcal{C}$ that are connected to $\mathcal{G}_h$ through a limited number of links [21]. This meta-definition relies on a locality principle in the expansion of a community, whereby constraining the portion of diffusion graph conditional to the target lurkers is performed through the expansion of their communities with adjacent ones. Two main types of expansion are recognized [21] (cf. Chap. 7 for the definitions of in-bridge and out-bridge):

- the *weakly-knit expanded community* for $\mathcal{G}_h$, denoted with $\mathcal{G} \sqsupseteq_w \mathcal{G}_h$, is defined as the subgraph obtained by connecting $\mathcal{G}_h$ to each community graph $\mathcal{G}_j, h \neq j$, such that there exists an *in-bridge* $(u, v) \in \mathcal{E}$ for $\mathcal{G}_h$, with $u \in \mathcal{V}_j$.
- the *tightly-knit expanded community* for $\mathcal{G}_h$, denoted with $\mathcal{G} \sqsupseteq_t \mathcal{G}_h$, is defined as the subgraph obtained by connecting to $\mathcal{G}_h$ each community graph $\mathcal{G}_j, h \neq j$, such that there exists an *in-bridge* $(u, v) \in \mathcal{E}$ for $\mathcal{G}_h$, and one of the following conditions hold:

  - there exists an *out-bridge* $(v', u) \in \mathcal{E}$ for $\mathcal{G}_h$, with $u \in \mathcal{V}_j$;
  - there exists an *out-bridge* $(v', u') \in \mathcal{E}$ for $\mathcal{G}_h$, with $u, u' \in \mathcal{V}_j$, and u' linked to u through a path in $\mathcal{G}_j$.

Figure 6.1 shows the outcome of applying the above defined community-expansion notions to a community containing a single target node (the filled circle) [21]. The weakly-knit expansion involves a community that is adjacent to the one containing the target through at least one incoming edge from it to the target's community (Fig. 6.1a). The tightly-knit expansion requires higher connectivity,

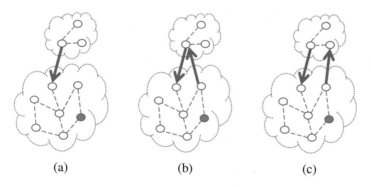

(a)   (b)   (c)

Fig. 6.1 Illustration of expanded community: (**a**) example of weakly-knit expansion, (**b**)–(**c**) examples of tightly-knit expansion [21]

since nodes at the boundary of the target's community and nodes at the boundary of an adjacent community must be linked through at least one pair of incoming and outgoing edge (Fig. 6.1b, c).

Both definitions of community expansion can be generalized in order to determine *recursively expanded* communities, which leads to the linkage of communities through a given number of bridges; formally, for any integer $D \geq 1$, the *D-recursively expanded community* for $\mathcal{G}_h$ is defined as $\mathcal{G}_h \cup EC^{(1)} \cup \ldots \cup EC^{(D)}$, where $EC^{(i)} = \{\mathcal{G} \in \mathcal{C} | \mathcal{G} \sqsupseteq \mathcal{G}', \mathcal{G}' \in EC^{(i-1)}\}$ (with $i = 2..D$), and $EC^{(1)} = \{\mathcal{G} \in \mathcal{C} | \mathcal{G} \sqsupseteq \mathcal{G}_h\}$ [21]. Note that symbol $\sqsupseteq$ refers to either $\sqsupseteq_w$ or $\sqsupseteq_t$, since a D-recursively expanded community can be defined according to both weakly- and tightly-knit expansion notions.

Algorithm 3 sketches the community-based DEvOTION workflow [21], which incorporates the previously described notions of expanded community graphs. The algorithm takes as input an information diffusion graph $\mathcal{G}$, a community structure $\mathcal{C}$ defined over $\mathcal{G}$, the DEvOTION parameters (i.e., size k of seed set, lurking threshold LS for the selection of the target set, and path pruning threshold η), and an integer D that defines the shortest path length between adjacent communities used in the recursive expansion of community. Moreover, symbols **WF1–WF4** denote the possible contingencies of usage of any given community graph as diffusion context: no expansion (**WF1**), weakly-knit expansion (**WF2**), tightly-knit expansion (**WF3**), and recursively expansion (**WF4**).

Empirical evidence relating to an experimental evaluation of Algorithm 3 conducted by the authors in [21] has shown that the best active users for lurker engagement (i.e., the k seeds discovered by DEvOTION) are more likely to be identified among members of communities external to that of the target lurkers. Such external communities are adjacent to the community containing the targets, linked

---

Algorithm 3 Community-Based DEvOTION Workflow [21]

Input: An information diffusion graph $\mathcal{G} = \langle \mathcal{V}, \mathcal{E}, b, \ell \rangle$,
    a community structure $\mathcal{C} = \{\mathcal{G}_1, \ldots, \mathcal{G}_H\}$ over $\mathcal{G}$,
    a set of N seed-set size values $K = \{k_1, \ldots, k_N\}$,
    a set of M lurking threshold values $L = \{LS_1, \ldots, LS_M\}$ (with $LS_i \in [0, 1]$),
    a path pruning threshold $\eta \in [0, 1]$,
    an integer $D \geq 1$.
1: **for** $\mathcal{G}_h \in \mathcal{C}$ **do**
2:     **for** $LS_m \in L$ **do**
3:         Identify the target set $TS_{h,m}$ among nodes in $\mathcal{G}_h$
4:         **for** $k_n \in K$ **do**
5:             Apply DEvOTION with target set $TS_{h,m}$ and seed set size k_n, over:
6:             (**WF1**) the community graph $\mathcal{G}_h$
7:             (**WF2**) the weakly-knit expanded community graph of $\mathcal{G}_h$
8:             (**WF3**) the tightly-knit expanded community graph of $\mathcal{G}_h$
9:             (**WF4**) the D-recursively expanded community graph of $\mathcal{G}_h$
10:         **end for**
11:     **end for**
12: **end for**

---

through bridges. Moreover, by expanding the community subgraph corresponding to the diffusion context, it is more likely to engage lurkers having high activation probability, i.e., users exhibiting a stronger lurking behavior. Also, the size of community tends to have a relatively low impact on the trends of the activation probability density distributions, which makes the approach robust against community structures of varying composition.

6.3.4 Diversity-Aware Delurking

As previously discussed, a key issue in (targeted) influence maximization applications concerns the budget constraint: while maximizing the advertising of a product, one also needs to minimize the incentives offered to those users who will reach out the target ones. This obviously raises the necessity of making an appropriate marketing investment in the form of the number k of initial influencers (seeds) to be detected. Nonetheless, one aspect that has been overlooked is that the success of the outcome of a viral marketing process might depend not only on the *size* of the seed set but also on the *diversity* that is reflected within, or in relation to, the seed set. Quoting from Scientific American [36],

> to build teams or organizations capable of innovating, you need diversity. Diversity enhances creativity. It encourages the search for novel information and perspectives, leading to better decision making and problem solving. It can improve the bottom line of companies and lead to unfettered discoveries and breakthrough innovations.

Roughly speaking, individuals that differ from each other in terms of kind (e.g., age, gender), socio-cultural aspects (e.g., nationality, race) or other characteristics, bring unique information, opinions, experiences, and perspectives to bear on the task at hand. This definitely reflects in an OSN context as well, where members naturally have different backgrounds, motivations for participation, and information to share [35, 38, 42]. One important implication here is that if on the one hand diverse users tend to connect to users of many different types, on the other hand the engagement of users who have not yet experienced community commitment, i.e., lurkers, can be more difficult if the triggering stimuli from the influential, active users are not sufficiently diversified.

6.3.4.1 Diversity in Information Spreading

Most existing notions of diversity have been developed around structural features of the network, or alternatively based on user profile attributes, in various research fields, including web search, recommendation systems, and information spreading. Focusing on the latter, the authors in [26] introduce several basic measures of diversity and show their evolution during the lifetime of the network. One of the measures they propose is controllability, defined as the number of nodes needed to control a network, i.e., nodes able to spread an opinion through the whole network. The latter is estimated by finding a maximal matching in the bipartite cover of the network. In [4], the IC model is extended to take into account the structural diversity of nodes' neighborhood. For each node in the graph, its neighborhood is computed as the union of components that in turn are defined as sets of its interconnected in-neighbors. A component-based diffusion process is defined and the tightness of connections within the component are exploited to infer the model parameters. The aforementioned works do not consider any optimization problem.

Other works deal with the problem of estimating the spreading ability of a single node in a network [10, 19]. In [10], the authors propose a measure that combines global diversity and local feature (e.g., degree centrality) to identify the most influential spreaders. The diversity is determined by computing the neighbors' position in the network, which can be obtained exploiting community detection or k-shell decomposition. Experiments have been conducted on several networks to assess the validity of this measure w.r.t. baselines (e.g., closeness and betweenness centrality), by modeling the diffusion process through the SIR epidemic model [33]. However, in their analysis, the authors consider only a single initial spreader, i.e., the most influential node. In general, it is worth noting that the problem of finding an optimal set of k influential nodes is different from the problem of selecting k nodes that are each individually optimal. Intuitively enough, if two top influential nodes both have strong influence on the same group of nodes, the influence exerted by this ensemble will be quite a bit less than the sum of the influence of each of the nodes. As a result, this measure, as well as any naive centrality measures, will likely fail to find the optimal set of influential nodes.

Node diversity into the influence maximization task has been introduced in [46]. Given a set of categories and the category distribution of each node, the authors propose a set of diversity measures that satisfy monotonicity and submodularity. The overall objective function, to be maximized w.r.t. both influence and diversity, is also submodular under the IC and LT models.

6.3.4.2   Diversity-Integrated Targeted Influence Maximization

In [7], the authors propose to embed a notion of diversity into the problem of targeted influence maximization. The underlying assumption in that study is as follows: if one learns seeds that are not only capable of spreading influence but also are linked to more diverse (groups of) users, then it is likely that the influence will be diversified as well, and hence the target users will get higher chance of being engaged. The proposed approach relies on taking a perspective that does not assume any side-information or a-priori knowledge on user attributes (e.g., personal profile, topical preference, community role, or any other dimension in a predetermined discrete domain) that can enable diversification among users. Rather, the authors assume that *a user's diversity in a social graph can be determined based on topological properties related to her/his neighborhood*, which finds justifications from social science theories of *social embeddedness* [16] and

Fig. 6.2 Effect of
topological diversity on the
outcome of targeted influence
maximization [7]

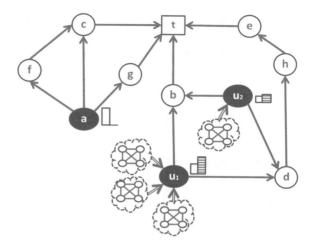

boundary spanning [1, 8, 43]—the former is seen as a manifestation of diversity
related to how well a user is connected to others within the online community,
whereas the latter explains how OSN users share and diffuse knowledge acquired
from their social contacts to other contacts that belong to different components of
the social graph (cf. Chap. 7).

To support the above hypothesis, consider the example social graph shown in
Fig. 6.2 and borrowed from [7], where nodes represent users and edges express
influence relationships in the context of a diffusion process, captured at a given
time step—both the influence probabilities as edge weights and the active/inactive
nodes are not indicated, for the sake of simplicity. Let us consider the target node
t, and assume that the colored nodes a, u_1, u_2 correspond to candidate seeds,
for which we know the following information: the individual cumulated spreading
influence towards t (indicated by the leftmost bar associated to each of the nodes)
and the individual topological diversity, according to some topology-driven notion
of diversity (indicated by the rightmost bar associated to each of the nodes). A
conventional method for targeted influence maximization would choose node a
as seed, since it has the highest capability of spread among the candidate seeds;
however, a's location likely corresponds to low topological diversity, because the
node does not receive any incoming connections from other components in the
graph, and it diffuses towards nodes that are all in the same subgraph having t
as sink. By contrast, the location of nodes u is strategical in terms of topological
diversity, since they could be influenced by one or more groups of nodes (in the
figure indicated as components enclosed within dashed clouds), thus potentially
acquiring a wider spectrum of varied information and perspectives. Selecting nodes
u would hence be favored by a diversity-aware targeted influence maximization
method as they might be more effective in increasing node t's engagement.

A novel problem, named ***Diversity-integrated Targeted Influence Maximization***
(DTIM) is formulated in [7] to bring the aforementioned concept of topology-
driven diversity into targeted influence maximization. Given a diffusion graph

$\mathscr{G} = \langle \mathscr{V}, \mathscr{E}, b, \ell \rangle$, a budget k, and a threshold $LS \in [0, 1]$, the **DTIM** problem is to find a seed set $S \subseteq \mathscr{V}$ with $|S| \le k$ of users such that, by activating them, the *Diversity-Integrated Capital (DIC)* is maximized:

$$
\begin{aligned}
S &= \underset{S' \subseteq \mathscr{V} \ s.t. \ |S'| \le k}{\operatorname{argmax}} \quad DIC \\
&= \underset{S' \subseteq \mathscr{V} \ s.t. \ |S'| \le k}{\operatorname{argmax}} \quad \alpha DC(\mu(S')) + (1 - \alpha)D(S')
\end{aligned}
\tag{6.5}
$$

where the target set corresponding to the user-specified threshold LS is $TS = \{v \in \mathscr{V} \mid \ell(v) \ge LS\}$, and

- for any $S \subseteq \mathscr{V}$, $DC(\mu(S))$ is the *capital* associated with the final active set $\mu(S)$:

$$
DC(\mu(S)) = \sum_{v \in (\mu(S) \cap TS) \setminus S} \ell(v)
\tag{6.6}
$$

- for any $S \subseteq \mathscr{V}$, $D(S)$ is the *diversity* associated with the target set $TS \subseteq \mathscr{V}$:

$$
D(S) = \sum_{s \in S} \sum_{t \in TS} div_t(s)
\tag{6.7}
$$

- $\alpha \in [0, 1]$ is a smoothing parameter that controls the weight of capital DC with respect to diversity D.

The objective function of the **DTIM** problem is hence a linear combination of two functions, *capital* and *diversity*. The former is determined as proportional to the cumulative status of the target users that are activated by the seed set S, whereas the latter captures the overall diversity of the users in S w.r.t. the target set, by aggregating the individual diversity through the div_t function. The authors define two alternative ways of modeling the div_t function, which differ in the exploitation of the structural information from the diffusion subgraph specific to a given target node. (A target-specific diffusion subgraph corresponds the portion of the diffusion graph involved, at a given time step, in the unfolding of the diffusion towards a particular target node.) The first method, dubbed *local diversity*, computes at each step of the expansion of a target-specific diffusion subgraph, the user diversity as the likelihood of reaching it from users outside the currently unfolded target-specific diffusion subgraph. The second method of topology-driven diversity, dubbed *global diversity*, exploits the structural information of the fully unfolded target-specific diffusion subgraph, and determines the diversity of nodes that lay on the boundary of the subgraph, i.e., nodes that can receive influence links from nodes external to the subgraph; here the intuition is to capture a boundary-spanning effect of external sources of influence coming from the rest of the social graph.

The objective function of the **DTIM** problem is proved to be monotone and submodular, since it is a non-negative linear combination of two functions that are in turn monotone and submodular [7]. Upon this result, the authors provide both a greedy approximation algorithm and a RIS-based approximation for the DTIM problem [7].

References

1. Boundary spanning. In R. Alhajj and J. Rokne, editors, *Encyclopedia of Social Network Analysis and Mining*, page 82. 2014.
2. Ç. Aslay, W. Lu, F. Bonchi, A. Goyal, and L. V. S. Lakshmanan. Viral marketing meets social advertising: Ad allocation with minimum regret. *PVLDB*, 8(7):822–833, 2015.
3. E. Bakshy, I. Rosenn, C. Marlow, and L. A. Adamic. The role of social networks in information diffusion. In *Proc. World Wide Web Conf. (WWW)*, pages 519–528, 2012.
4. Q. Bao, W. K. Cheung, and Y. Zhang. Incorporating structural diversity of neighbors in a diffusion model for social networks. In *Proc. IEEE/WIC/ACM Int. Conf. on Web Intelligence*, pages 431–438, 2013.
5. Nicola Barbieri, Fabrizio Silvestri, and Mounia Lalmas. Improving post-click user engagement on native ads via survival analysis. In *Proceedings of the 25th International Conference on World Wide Web, WWW 2016, Montreal, Canada, April 11-15, 2016*, pages 761–770, 2016.
6. F. Bonchi. Influence propagation in social networks: A data mining perspective. *IEEE Intelligent Informatics Bulletin*, 12(1):8–16, 2011.
7. A. Caliò, R. Interdonato, C. Pulice, and A. Tagarelli. Topology-driven diversity for targeted influence maximization with application to user engagement in social networks. *IEEE Transactions on Knowledge and Data Engineering*, 2018.
8. J. Cranefield, P. Yoong, and S. L. Huff. Beyond Lurking: The Invisible Follower-Feeder In An Online Community Ecosystem. In *Proc. Pacific Asia Conf. on Information Systems (PACIS)*, page 50, 2011.
9. Ali Darejeh and Siti Salwah Salim. Gamification solutions to enhance software user engagement - A systematic review. *Int. J. Hum. Comput. Interaction*, 32(8):613–642, 2016.
10. Y.-H. Fu, C.-Y. Huang, and C.-T. Sun. Using global diversity and local topology features to identify influential network spreaders. *Physica A: Statistical Mechanics and its Applications*, 433(C):344–355, 2015.
11. Paul Michael Di Gangi and Molly McLure Wasko. Social media engagement theory: Exploring the influence of user engagement on social media usage. *JOEUC*, 28(2):53–73, 2016.
12. A. Goyal, W. Lu, and L. V. S. Lakshmanan. SIMPATH: An Efficient Algorithm for Influence Maximization under the Linear Threshold Model. In *Proc. IEEE Int. Conf. on Data Mining (ICDM)*, pages 211–220, 2011.
13. A. Guille, H. Hacid, C. Favre, and D. A. Zighed. Information diffusion in online social networks: a survey. *SIGMOD Record*, 42(2):17–28, 2013.
14. B. Guler, B. Varan, K. Tutuncuoglu, M. S. Nafea, A. A. Zewail, A. Yener, and D. Octeau. Optimal strategies for targeted influence in signed networks. In *Proc. Int. Conf. on Advances in Social Networks Analysis and Mining (ASONAM)*, pages 906–911, 2014.
15. J. Guo, P. Zhang, C. Zhou, Y. Cao, and L. Guo. Personalized influence maximization on social networks. In *Proc. ACM Conf. on Information and Knowledge Management (CIKM)*, pages 199–208, 2013.
16. D. A. Harrison and K. J. Klein. What's the difference? diversity constructs as separation, variety, or disparity in organizations. *Academy of Management Review*, 32:1199–1228, 2007.
17. Nathan O. Hodas, Ryan Butner, and Courtney Corley. How a user's personality influences content engagement in social media. In *Social Informatics - 8th International Conference, SocInfo 2016, Bellevue, WA, USA, November 11-14, 2016, Proceedings, Part I*, pages 481–493, 2016.

18. Yuheng Hu, Shelly Farnham, and Kartik Talamadupula. Predicting user engagement on twitter with real-world events. In *Proceedings of the Ninth International Conference on Web and Social Media, ICWSM 2015, University of Oxford, Oxford, UK, May 26-29, 2015*, pages 168–178, 2015.

19. P.-Y. Huang, H.-Y. Liu, C.-H. Chen, and P.-J. Cheng. The impact of social diversity and dynamic influence propagation for identifying influencers in social networks. In *Proc. IEEE/WIC/ACM Int. Conf. on Web Intelligence*, pages 410–416, 2013.

20. R. Interdonato, C. Pulice, and A. Tagarelli. "Got to have faith!": The DEvOTION algorithm for delurking in social networks. In *Proc. Int. Conf. on Advances in Social Networks Analysis and Mining (ASONAM)*, pages 314–319, 2015.

21. R. Interdonato, C. Pulice, and A. Tagarelli. Community-based delurking in social networks. In *Proc. Int. Conf. on Advances in Social Networks Analysis and Mining (ASONAM)*, 2016.

22. Roberto Interdonato, Chiara Pulice, and Andrea Tagarelli. *The DEvOTION Algorithm for Delurking in Social Networks*, pages 77–106. Springer International Publishing, 2017.

23. D. Kempe, J. M. Kleinberg, and E. Tardos. Maximizing the spread of influence through a social network. In *Proc. ACM SIGKDD Int. Conf. on Knowledge Discovery and Data Mining (KDD)*, pages 137–146, 2003.

24. M. Laeeq Khan. Social media engagement: What motivates user participation and consumption on youtube? *Computers in Human Behavior*, 66:236–247, 2017.

25. Hamid Khobzi and Babak Teimourpour. LCP segmentation: A framework for evaluation of user engagement in online social networks. *Computers in Human Behavior*, 50:101–107, 2015.

26. J. Kunegis, S. Sizov, F. Schwagereit, and D. Fay. Diversity dynamics in online networks. In *Proc. ACM Conf. on Hypertext and Social Media (HT)*, pages 255–264, 2012.

27. H.-M. Lai and T. T. Chen. Knowledge sharing in interest online communities: A comparison of posters and lurkers. *Computers in Human Behavior*, 35:295–306, 2014.

28. H. Li, S. S. Bhowmick, A. Sun, and J. Cui. Conformity-aware influence maximization in online social networks. *The VLDB Journal*, 24:117–141, 2015.

29. Y. Li, D. Zhang, and K.-L. Tan. Real-time targeted influence maximization for online advertisements. *PVLDB*, 8(10):1070–1081, 2015.

30. Leora Mauda and Yoram M. Kalman. Characterizing quantitative measures of user engagement on organizational facebook pages. In *49th Hawaii International Conference on System Sciences, HICSS 2016, Koloa, HI, USA, January 5-8, 2016*, pages 3526–3535, 2016.

31. A. Nazi, M. Das, and G. Das. The TagAdvisor: Luring the Lurkers to Review Web Items. In *Proc. ACM SIGMOD Int. Conf. on Management of Data (SIGMOD)*, pages 531–543, 2015.

32. M. E. J. Newman and M. Girvan. Finding and evaluating community structure in networks. *Phys. Rev. E*, 69(2):026113, 2004.

33. Mark Newman. *Networks: An Introduction*. Oxford University Press, Inc., New York, NY, USA, 2010.

34. Heather O'Brien and Paul A. Cairns. An empirical evaluation of the user engagement scale (UES) in online news environments. *Inf. Process. Manage.*, 51(4):413–427, 2015.

35. Z. Pan, Y. Lu, and S. Gupta. How heterogeneous community engage newcomers? The effect of community diversity on newcomers' perception of inclusion: An empirical study in social media service. *Computers in Human Behavior*, 39:100–111, 2014.

36. K. W. Phillips. How diversity makes us smarter. *Scientific American*, 311(4), October 2014.

37. Soumya Ray, Sung S. Kim, and James G. Morris. The central role of engagement in online communities. *Information Systems Research*, 25(3):528–546, 2014.

38. L. Robert and D. M. Romero. Crowd size, diversity and performance. In *Proc. ACM Conf. on Human Factors in Computing Systems (CHI)*, pages 1379–1382, 2015.

39. Giulio Rossetti, Luca Pappalardo, Riivo Kikas, Dino Pedreschi, Fosca Giannotti, and Marlon Dumas. Community-centric analysis of user engagement in Skype social network. In *Proc. Int. Conf. on Advances in Social Networks Analysis and Mining (ASONAM)*, pages 547–552, 2015.

40. K. Saito, K. Ohara, Y. Yamagishi, M. Kimura, and H. Motoda. Learning Diffusion Probability Based on Node Attributes in Social Networks. In *Proc. Int. Symposium on Methodologies for Intelligent Systems (ISMIS)*, pages 153–162, 2011.

41. Shumpei Sano, Nobuhiro Kaji, and Manabu Sassano. Prediction of prospective user engagement with intelligent assistants. In *Proceedings of the 54th Annual Meeting of the Association for Computational Linguistics, ACL 2016, August 7-12, 2016, Berlin, Germany, Volume 1: Long Papers*, 2016.
42. F. C. Santos, M. D. Santos, and J.M. Pacheco. Social diversity promotes the emergence of cooperation in public goods games. *Nature*, 454:231–216, 2008.
43. V. Soroka and S. Rafaeli. Invisible participants: how cultural capital relates to lurking behavior. In *Proc. ACM Conf. on World Wide Web (WWW)*, pages 163–172, 2006.
44. N. Sun, P. P.-L. Rau, and L. Ma. Understanding lurkers in online communities: a literature review. *Computers in Human Behavior*, 38:110–117, 2014.
45. A. Tagarelli and R. Interdonato. Lurking in social networks: topology-based analysis and ranking methods. *Social Netw. Analys. Mining*, 4(230):27, 2014.
46. F. Tang, Q. Liu, H. Zhu, E. Chen, and F. Zhu. Diversified social influence maximization. In *Proc. Int. Conf. on Advances in Social Networks Analysis and Mining (ASONAM)*, pages 455–459, 2014.
47. L. Tang and H. Liu. *Community detection and mining in social media*. Synthesis Lectures on Data Mining and Knowledge Discovery, Morgan & Claypool, 2010.
48. Y. Tang, X. Xiao, and Y. Shi. Influence maximization: near-optimal time complexity meets practical efficiency. In *Proc. ACM SIGMOD Int. Conf. on Management of Data (SIGMOD)*, pages 75–86, 2014.
49. D. J. Watts. A simple model of global cascades on random networks. *PNAS*, 99:5766–5771, 2002.
50. L. Weng, J. Ratkiewicz, N. Perra, B. Gonçalves, C. Castillo, F. Bonchi, R. Schifanella, F. Menczer, and A. Flammini. The role of information diffusion in the evolution of social networks. In *Proc. ACM SIGKDD Int. Conf. on Knowledge Discovery and Data Mining (KDD)*, pages 356–364, 2013.
51. D.-N. Yang, H.-J. Hung, Wa.-C. Lee, and W. Chen. Maximizing acceptance probability for active friending in online social networks. In *Proc. ACM SIGKDD Int. Conf. on Knowledge Discovery and Data Mining (KDD)*, pages 713–721, 2013.
52. Xiabing Zheng, Christy M. K. Cheung, Matthew K. O. Lee, and Liang Liang. Building brand loyalty through user engagement in online brand communities in social networking sites. *IT & People*, 28(1):90–106, 2015.

Chapter 7
Boundary Spanning Lurking

Abstract The social boundary spanning theory explains how OSN users share and transfer their knowledge through the network. In this chapter, we consider two aspects related to the role of lurkers in boundary spanning contexts. In the first part, we concentrate on the relation between lurkers and OSN communities, discussing how the user's capability of across-community boundary spanning can relate with the role s/he may take in the community, and to what extent lurkers match community-based bridge users. In the second part, we introduce the problem of alternate lurker-contributor behaviors, under a framework of multilayer network modeling cross-platform user behaviors, and describe solutions based on ranking methods.

Social interactions between individuals naturally favor the propagation of knowledge through different communities. In this context, the *social boundary spanning theory* [1, 3] describes the way OSN users naturally redistribute the knowledge they acquire from their social contacts to different components of a social network. Under this perspective, a privileged position is that taken by users laying on the boundary of a component, since they usually play the role of *bridges* over different components.

Influential contributor users can naturally act as knowledge-spreading bridges, as studied in [7, 11, 12]. However, due to their behavior and to their position in the network, lurkers have a strong relation with users acting as bridges between communities too, as anticipated in Chap. 4. A preliminary analysis about this relation has been carried out by the authors in [10], through percolation analysis based on directed topological overlap.

Being exposed to the valuable knowledge produced by other (influential) OSN members belonging to different communities, lurkers can build their own perspective and start exploiting the acquired knowledge outside their own social circle, i.e., spreading it towards different communities or even different OSNs.

In this chapter, we focus on two aspects related to the role of lurkers in boundary spanning contexts. In Sect. 7.1, we enhance our understanding of the relation between lurkers and OSN communities, discussing how the across-community boundary spanning capability of a user relates with the role she/he takes in its community, and to what extent lurkers match community-based bridge users. In Sect. 7.2, we introduce the problem of alternate lurker-contributor behaviors. This builds on the assumptions that the social boundary spanning theory can be modeled in a multilayer network context, where different layers correspond to the boundaries in the complex system, and that users having accounts in multiple OSN platforms can take different, even opposite roles from one network to another.

7.1 Lurkers Across Communities

In this section we investigate relations between lurkers and OSN communities. Following the study in [4], we focus on two main aspects of this relation: (i) how users taking the role of bridge across communities are in relation with users taking an influential or prestigious role within a community, and (ii) what relations exist between bridge users and lurkers.

Let $\mathscr{C} = \{\mathscr{G}_1, \ldots, \mathscr{G}_H\}$ be a community structure defined over the information diffusion graph $\mathscr{G} = \langle \mathcal{V}, \mathcal{E}, b, \ell \rangle$, where each $\mathscr{G}_h = \langle \mathcal{V}_h, \mathcal{E}_h, b_h, \ell_h \rangle$, $h \in [1, H]$, denotes the directed weighted graph associated to the h-th community. Each $\mathscr{G}_h$ is an induced subgraph of $\mathscr{G}$, where $\mathcal{V}_h \subseteq \mathcal{V}$ and $\mathcal{E}_h \subseteq \mathcal{E}$ contains all edges of $\mathcal{E}$ connecting two nodes in $\mathcal{V}_h$.

Given a community structure $\mathscr{C}$, and subgraphs $\mathscr{G}_h, \mathscr{G}_j$ corresponding to the h-th and j-th community in $\mathscr{C}$, respectively, let $v \in \mathcal{V}_h$ and $u \in \mathcal{V}_j$. Edge $(u, v) \in \mathcal{E}$ is said *in-bridge* for community $\mathscr{G}_h$ and *out-bridge* for community $\mathscr{G}_j$. Moreover, node v is said *in-bridge node* for $\mathscr{G}_h$, and node u is said *out-bridge node* for $\mathscr{G}_j$.

7.1.1 Across-Community Boundary Spanning vs. Within-Community Centrality

The analysis carried out in [4] takes into account two aspects in order to describe the relation between users bridging different communities and their role within a community: (i) the property of each node of being a good "bridge" between its own community and other communities, and (ii) the status of the node of being "prestigious" within the community it belongs to. The first aspect is quantified by calculating the number of in-bridges, otherwise out-bridges, associated with each node. The second aspect is instead addressed by means of a centrality measure contextually applied to each particular community-induced subgraph. The authors in [4] resort to PageRank [2] to calculate the prestige of each node of a community-induced subgraph (i.e., a user is important if s/he is endorsed by other important users). It is important to point out that the prestige scores are determined on the *lurking-oriented* topology (see Sect. 3.1), i.e., an edge (v, u) means that u is "consuming" or "receiving" information from v (that is, v influences u).

The authors in [4] analyze for each community, two distributions over the community nodes: the distribution of the number of in-bridges (resp. out-bridges) incident in each node and the distribution of the prestige rank of each node. Communities are determined using the state-of-the-art *Infomap* algorithm [9] for community detection, which inherently provides a ranking score of the prestige that nodes have within their community. By carrying out experiments on three real-world networks (namely, *FriendFeed*, *GooglePlus*, and *Instagram*), the authors in [4] show how the two aspects are generally negatively correlated, both when considering the distribution over all the community nodes and the distribution over a fraction of top-lurkers (i.e., top-5%, top-10%, and top-25% lurkers as ranked by LurkerRank). This indicates that the prestige of users within the community they belong to is negatively related to both in-bridging and out-bridging property of the users. In other terms, users that are important within their community might significantly differ from those users that span across communities, through both inward and outward connections [4].

7.1.2 Lurkers vs. Community-Based Bridge Users

The second part of the analysis in [4] is devoted to the study of the relations between bridge users and lurkers, based on the analysis of the matching between bridge-nodes and top-ranked lurkers. Experimental results obtained on *FriendFeed*, *GooglePlus* and *Instagram* networks, show that the fraction of lurkers that are in-bridge nodes is very high on all datasets (always above 85%, with peaks of nearly 100%). Moreover, the fraction of bridge nodes that are top-lurkers is significant even for top-5% lurkers (between 6 and 10%), up to 33–44% for top-25% lurkers. Different situation occurs when considering out-bridges, with much lower values than those observed for the in-bridge evaluation. Summing up, lurkers are more likely to match in-bridge users than out-bridge users. This would imply that lurkers are more likely to acquire information from outside their own community than to spread information towards other communities [4].

7.2 Cross-OSN Analysis of Alternate Behaviors of Lurking and Active Participation

We have previously discussed how the social boundary spanning theory can help describe the role of lurkers lying at the edge between different communities in an OSN. Here we will extend this concept to a cross-OSN scenario.

Nowadays, it is extremely common for a user to own profiles on different OSNs. Even belonging to the same physical user, these different profiles are associated to (generally) different relation sets, and consequently to different knowledge and influence sources. This context implies that the same user is likely to play different roles on different OSNs, i.e., s/he may be lurker on certain OSNs, and being an active contributor on other OSNs, thus partially redistributing the knowledge absorbed from the OSNs where s/he lurks.

The study proposed in [8] models a cross-OSN scenario as a multilayer network, where each layer corresponds to a different OSN. The aim of the authors is to understand how the knowledge flows across different layers of a complex network, by studying the behavior of users which may alternately take the role of contributors and lurkers over different layer networks. To support the study of the dichotomy between information-producers (i.e., contributors) and information-consumers (i.e., lurkers) and their interplay over a multilayer network, the authors propose a multilayer ranking method, namely mIALCR, able to identify and rank alternate lurker-contributor behaviors on a multilayer OSN. In the subsequent sections we will describe in detail the approach proposed in [8].

7.2.1 Multilayer Network Model

Let $\mathscr{L} = \{L_1, \ldots, L_\ell\}$ be a set of *layers*, with $\ell \geq 2$. Each layer corresponds to a particular user relational context. Given a set $\mathscr{V}$ of *entities* or *actors* (i.e., users), for each choice of user in $\mathscr{V}$ and layer in $\mathscr{L}$, we need to indicate whether the user is present in that layer. We denote with $V_{\mathscr{L}} \subseteq \mathscr{V} \times \mathscr{L}$ the set containing the user-layer combinations (i.e., tuples) in which a user is present in the corresponding layer. The set $E_{\mathscr{L}} \subseteq V_{\mathscr{L}} \times V_{\mathscr{L}}$ contains the *directed links* between user-layer tuples. Note that, when all layers refer to the same aspect or dimension like in our setting, the elements in $V_{\mathscr{L}}$ simply correspond to pairs ⟨*node, layer*⟩. We denote with $G_{\mathscr{L}} = (V_{\mathscr{L}}, E_{\mathscr{L}}, \mathscr{V}, \mathscr{L})$ the *multilayer network graph* with set of entities $\mathscr{V}$ and set of layers $\mathscr{L}$.

For every layer $L_i \in \mathscr{L}$, let $V_{L_i} = \bigcup_{v \in \mathscr{V}} (v, L_i)$ be the set of pairs expressing the occurrences of entities in the graph of L_i, and $E_{L_i} \subseteq V_{L_i} \times V_{L_i}$ be the set of edges in L_i; to simplify notations, we will also refer to V_{L_i} and E_{L_i} as V_i and E_i, respectively. Moreover, we will use notation $v \in V_i$ to indicate $v \in \mathscr{V}$ s.t. $\exists (v, L_i) \in V_i$. For any node $v \in V_i$, we denote with $N_i^{in}(v) = \{u \in V_i | ((u, L_i), (v, L_i)) \in E_i\}$ the set of nodes that are in-neighbors of v within the same layer of v, and with $N_{\neg i}^{in}(v) = \bigcup_{j \neq i} \{u \in V_j | (u, L_j), (v, L_j) \in E_j\}$ the set of nodes that are in-neighbors of v within any of the other layers. Analogous definitions hold for the out-neighbor sets $N_i^{out}(v)$ and $N_{\neg i}^{out}(v)$ [8].

Note that while entities (i.e., elements of $\mathscr{V}$) are not required to participate in all layers, each entity has to appear in at least one layer. Moreover, the only inter-layer edges are regarded as "couplings" of nodes representing the same entity between different layers, according to a multiplex network representation.

7.2.2 Multilayer LurkerRank

Before presenting the mlALCR algorithms, the authors in [8] also define a multilayer extension of the original LurkerRank, dubbed mlLR. More specifically, they extend the formulation of the *in-out-neighbors-driven lurker ranking* (see Sect. 3.2) to deal with multiple layers. Following the lead of [5], the key idea is to make the underlying random-walk model be expressed by as many transition probability matrices as the different layers. These matrices are then linearly combined, using a proper weighting scheme (e.g., weights following a probability distribution, or reflecting some user preference or knowledge on the relevance of the various layers) [8].

Given a multilayer graph $G_{\mathscr{L}} = (V_{\mathscr{L}}, E_{\mathscr{L}}, \mathscr{V}, \mathscr{L})$, the *multilayer LurkerRank*, hereinafter denoted as mlLR, is defined by the following system of equations, for all $v \in \mathscr{V}$ [8]:

$$\mathsf{mlLR}(v) = d[\mathscr{R}^{\text{in}}(v)\,(1 + \mathscr{R}^{\text{out}}(v))] + (1-d)p(v) \qquad (7.1)$$

with

$$\mathscr{R}^{\text{in}}(v) = \sum_{L_i \in \mathscr{L}} \frac{\omega_i}{|N_i^{out}(v)|} \sum_{u \in N_i^{in}(v)} \frac{|N_i^{out}(u)|}{|N_i^{in}(u)|}\mathsf{mlLR}(u) \qquad (7.2)$$

$$\mathscr{R}^{\text{out}}(v) = \sum_{L_i \in \mathscr{L}} \frac{\omega_i|N_i^{in}(v)|}{\sum_{u \in N_i^{out}(v)} |N_i^{in}(u)|} \sum_{u \in N_i^{out}(v)} \frac{|N_i^{in}(u)|}{|N_i^{out}(u)|}\mathsf{mlLR}(u) \qquad (7.3)$$

where d denotes a damping factor ranging within [0,1], and the layer weights are specified by non-negative real-valued coefficients $\omega_1, \ldots, \omega_\ell$, such that $\sum_{L_i \in \mathscr{L}} \omega_i = 1$. Note that, with the exception of the specification of layer in the summation terms and the layer-specific weighting coefficient (for the linear combination), the analytical forms Eqs. (7.2) and (7.3) in mlLR are identical to those of the basic LurkerRank method presented in Sect. 3.2.

7.2.3 Multilayer Alternate Lurker-Contributor Ranking

The mlLR method is shown to be able to identify and rank lurking behaviors by exploiting the full multilayer network (i.e., detecting properties that would not emerge by analyzing each layer separately). However, it is not designed to identify and rank users according to opposite behaviors (i.e., lurker vs. contributor) they can alternately show over interconnected layer networks.

We report here the motivating example presented in [8] to illustrate the requirements and intuitions that prompted the authors to formulate a new ranking problem in multilayer networks, named *Alternate Lurker-Contributor Ranking*, based on an unsupervised learning approach.

Example 7.1 Consider the example multilayer social network shown in Fig. 7.1. We might suppose that layers correspond to three distinct OSNs to which users participate using their respective multiple accounts. We use symbols L_1, L_2, L_3 to denote the layers, from left to right. The meaning of edge (u, v) on any layer is that v endorses u, or consumes information produced by u (e.g., v follows u, or v likes/comments contents posted by u, etc.).

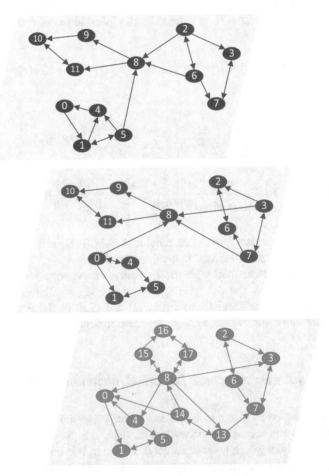

Fig. 7.1 Example multilayer social network, which illustrates eighteen users located over three layer networks [8]

At first, let us focus on simple topological characteristics, particularly on the ratio between in-neighbors and out-neighbors (hereinafter in/out-degree ratio) the nodes have on each of the layers. In L_1, users 2, 5 and, 6 appear to behave as contributors, since their in/out-degree ratio is lower than one (i.e., 0.33); by contrast, users 3, 4, 7, 10, 11 and 8 are potential lurkers since their in/out-degree is equal to 2. In L_2, users 1, 2, 5, 6, 10, 11 have the highest in/out-degree ratio (i.e., 2), so they are candidate lurkers in this specific layer. While users 0, 3, 7, 4 have the lowest ratio, and hence should be regarded as contributors. In L_3, candidate contributors are 13, 2, 4, 6, 14, 8 with in/out-degree ratio greater than one, while candidate lurkers are 0, 3, 7 with in/out-degree ratio equal to 3, and 1, 5, 15 with in/out-degree ratio equal to 2.

As previously discussed, there is however much more to be considered than the in/out-degree ratio to effectively analyze lurking behaviors, and dually, contributor behaviors), which further complicates in a multilayer network. For instance, user 8 receives information from two main components while providing limited information to a smaller component in L_1 and L_2, thus behaving as a lurker. By contrast, it is evident that the same user in L_3 acts as a major contributor by feeding various components; while not being the most active user in the layer (he is only the 6th if we consider the in/out degree ratio), user 8 might have the most distinctive alternate behavior in the multilayer network.

Also, user 3 receives information from her/his membership component in layer L_1 (which includes a local top-contributor such as 2), while in layer L_3 is fed by users 2, 7, and above all by the top-contributor user 8. By contrast, in L_2, user is top-contributor in her/his turn, as s/he receives information only from user 7 and feeds her/his component and user 8. Therefore, user 3 seems to show an important alternate behavior, which is strengthened by the effect of linkage to top-contributors/lurkers in all the three layers, and also nicely dovetails with the alternate behavior of user 8.

As another example, user 0 plays a marginal role in layer L_1, where she has only one outgoing link and one incoming link both limited to her/his component, and so s/he should not be identified either as a relevant lurker or contributor. Nevertheless, in the other layers s/he shows a different role: in L_3, s/he receives information from her/his own component, from user 8 and from previously unseen user 14; in L_2, s/he provides information to user 8 and towards her/his component.

The basic assumption in [8] is that the lurker (resp. contributor) status of a user relies on the contributor (resp. lurker) status of some of her/his neighbors. Upon this, the key idea underlying the approach is to determine the lurker and contributor behaviors of users in terms of two functions, each of which characterizes one role and is contextualized to a specific layer. This behavior is expected to be "alternated" over the various layers, in the sense that a user may act as a lurker (resp. contributor) in one layer while conversely behaving as a contributor (resp. lurker) in one or many of the other layers. Moreover, since the two behavioral properties are inter-related, the scores determined by one function depend on the scores by the other function [8].

Let $G_{\mathscr{L}} = (V_{\mathscr{L}}, E_{\mathscr{L}}, \mathscr{V}, \mathscr{L})$ be a multilayer OSN graph, and let us consider any user in $\mathscr{V}$ that appears in a non-empty, non-singleton subset of $\mathscr{L}$. Let $v \in V_{\mathscr{L}}$ denote the particular instance of the user in a specific layer $L_i \in \mathscr{L}$. The *alternate lurker-contributor behavior* status of node v in $G_{\mathscr{L}}$ conditionally to its membership layer L_i follows two principles, each expressed by two mutually reinforcing terms:

- *Principle 1—Cross-layer lurker behavior*, whose strength is proportional to the v's status as lurker in L_i, and to the v's status as contributor in a non-empty subset L' of layers other than L_i;
- *Principle 2—Cross-layer contributor behavior*, whose strength is proportional to the v's status as contributor in L_i, and to the v's status as lurker in a non-empty subset L'' of layers other than L_i;

More formally, by denoting with ϕ^L and ϕ^C two scoring functions respectively for the lurker and contributor status of nodes conditionally to a given (set of) layers, we want to determine the ranking solutions $rank^L$ and $rank^C$, such that for any $v \in V_{\mathscr{L}}$ in $L_i \in \mathscr{L}$:

- $rank^L(v)$ increases by simultaneously increasing $\phi^L(v; L_i, \phi^C)$ and $\phi^C(v; L', \phi^L)$,
- $rank^C(v)$ increases by simultaneously increasing $\phi^C(v; L_i, \phi^L)$ and $\phi^L(v; L'', \phi^C)$,

where $L', L'' \subseteq \mathscr{L} \setminus \{L_i\}$.

Upon the above stated problem, the authors in [8] define the *Alternate Lurker-Contributor Ranking* method (mlALCR), which solves two mutually dependent systems of equations that are computed simultaneously (in the style of classic Kleinberg's HITS algorithm for the ranking of hubs and authorities in web pages [6]): one system determines the layer-specific lurking score and the other system determines the layer-specific contributor score for all nodes in the layers of the complex network. According to the principles stated in the above definition, each of the role scoring functions (i.e., equation systems) is devised as a linear combination of two terms: the one measuring the user's behavior locally to her/his membership layer, and the other measuring the opposite behavior the same user might show externally to her/his membership layer.

Given a multilayer graph $G_{\mathscr{L}} = (V_{\mathscr{L}}, E_{\mathscr{L}}, \mathscr{V}, \mathscr{L})$, each layer is modeled as a directed graph according to the lurking-oriented direction of edges, i.e., (u, v) means that v endorses u by implicitly consuming/receiving information from u. For any node $v \in V_{\mathscr{L}}$ located in layer $L_i \in \mathscr{L}$, the *cross-layer lurking score* of v w.r.t. L_i, denoted as $\mathscr{R}_i^{lurk}(v)$, is determined by two terms: the first term is proportional to the number of v's in-neighbors and their status as cross-layer contributor in L_i, and inversely proportional to the number of v's out-neighbors in L_i; the second term is proportional to the number of v's out-neighbors and their status as cross-layer lurker in each of the remaining layers L_j (with $j \neq i$), and inversely proportional to the number of v's in-neighbors in each L_j [8]:

$$\mathcal{R}_i^{lurk}(v) = \alpha_l \underbrace{\frac{\omega_i}{|N_i^{out}(v)|} \sum_{u \in N_i^{in}(v)} \frac{\mathcal{R}_i^{contrib}(u)}{|N_{\neg i}^{out}(u)|}}_{v \text{ as } lurker \text{ in } L_i} +$$

$$(1-\alpha_l) \underbrace{\sum_{L_j \in \mathcal{L}} \left[\frac{\omega_j}{|N_j^{in}(v)|} \sum_{u \in N_j^{out}(v)} \frac{\mathcal{R}_j^{lurk}(u)}{|N_i^{in}(u)|} \right]}_{v \text{ as } contributor \text{ in } L_j, \text{ with } j \neq i} \quad (7.4)$$

Dually, the *cross-layer contributor score* of v w.r.t. L_i, denoted as $\mathcal{R}_i^{contrib}(v)$, is determined by two terms: the first term is proportional to the number of v's out-neighbors and their status as cross-layer lurker in L_i, and inversely proportional to the number of v's in-neighbors in L_i; the second term is proportional to the number of v's in-neighbors and their status as cross-layer contributor in each of the remaining layers L_j (with $j \neq i$), and inversely proportional to the number of v's out-neighbors in each L_j [8]:

$$\mathcal{R}_i^{contrib}(v) = \alpha_c \underbrace{\frac{\omega_i}{|N_i^{in}(v)|} \sum_{u \in N_i^{out}(v)} \frac{\mathcal{R}_i^{lurk}(u)}{|N_{\neg i}^{in}(u)|}}_{v \text{ as } contributor \text{ in } L_i} +$$

$$(1-\alpha_c) \underbrace{\sum_{L_j \in \mathcal{L}} \left[\frac{\omega_j}{|N_j^{out}(v)|} \sum_{u \in N_j^{in}(v)} \frac{\mathcal{R}_j^{contrib}(u)}{|N_i^{out}(u)|} \right]}_{v \text{ as } lurker \text{ in } L_j, \text{ with } j \neq i} \quad (7.5)$$

In both Eqs. (7.4) and (7.5), $\alpha_l, \alpha_c \in (0, 1)$ are damping factors that control the contribution of the "within-layer" behavior against the "outside-layer" opposite behavior. Moreover, ω_i (with $L_i \in \mathcal{L}$) are non-negative coefficients, such that $\sum_{L_i \in \mathcal{L}} \omega_i = 1$, which embed some relevance scheme that might be assigned to the various layers in the network. Note that, in order to avoid divergence of values, and hence guarantee convergence of the algorithm, both $\mathcal{R}^{lurk}$ and $\mathcal{R}^{contrib}$ score vectors are normalized after each iteration.

The authors in [8] conduct an experimental analysis on four real-world multilayer networks in order to assess performance of mIALCR from both a quantitatively and a qualitatively point of view. They also carry out a comparative evaluation against methods designed for ranking either contributors or lurkers.

mIALCR has shown to be able to identify users showing alternate behavior over the different layer networks. The results discussed in [8] reveal that lurker and contributor mIALCR solutions are clearly uncorrelated over the same network. When considering layer-specific projections of the solutions, there is a total disagreement in matching between the top-ranked users of C-mlALCR and L-mlALCR over the same layer, while correlation gets high for any pair of layers characterized by the presence of users with alternate lurker-contributor behavior. Empirical evidence based on manual inspection of top-ranked users has confirmed the ability of mlALCR in detecting users that simultaneously exhibit lurking behavior on one layer (e.g., OSN platform) while they spread the acquired knowledge acting as contributor on other layers, or vice versa.

As regards the comparison with baseline and competing methods presented in [8], within-layer lurkers identified by LurkerRank have generally no correlation (resp. strong mismatching) with cross-layer lurkers (resp. contributors) identified by mlALCR in the same layer. However, some correlation might be observed when lurkers in a given layer are likely to behave actively on other layers. Finally, top-ranked users in mlALCR and top-ranked users in the multilayer LurkerRank (mlLR) have no matching, while any positive correlation that may occur by comparing the entire ranking solutions depends on their respective tails.

References

1. Boundary spanning. In R. Alhajj and J. Rokne, editors, *Encyclopedia of Social Network Analysis and Mining*, page 82. 2014.
2. S. Brin and L. Page. The anatomy of a large-scale hypertextual Web search engine. *Computer Networks and ISDN Systems*, 30(1-7):107–117, 1998.
3. J. Cranefield, P. Yoong, and S. L. Huff. Beyond Lurking: The Invisible Follower-Feeder In An Online Community Ecosystem. In *Proc. Pacific Asia Conf. on Information Systems (PACIS)*, page 50, 2011.
4. R. Interdonato, C. Pulice, and A. Tagarelli. Community-based delurking in social networks. In *Proc. Int. Conf. on Advances in Social Networks Analysis and Mining (ASONAM)*, 2016.
5. R. Interdonato and A. Tagarelli. Multi-relational PageRank for tree structure sense ranking. *World Wide Web*, 18(5):1301–1329, 2015.
6. J. M. Kleinberg. Authoritative sources in a hyperlinked environment. *Journal of ACM*, 46(5):604–632, 1999.
7. A. J. Morales, J. C Losada, and R. M. Benito. Users structure and behavior on an online social network during a political protest. *Physica A*, 391(21):5244–5253, 2012.
8. Diego Perna, Roberto Interdonato, and Andrea Tagarelli. Identifying users with alternate behaviors of lurking and active participation in multilayer social networks. *IEEE Trans. Comput. Social Systems*, 5(1):46–63, 2018.
9. M. Rosvall and C. T. Bergstrom. Maps of random walks on complex networks reveal community structure. *Proc. Natl. Acad. Sci.*, page 1118, 2008.
10. A. Tagarelli and R. Interdonato. Lurking in social networks: topology-based analysis and ranking methods. *Social Netw. Analys. Mining*, 4(230):27, 2014.
11. H. Tong, S. Papadimitriou, C. Faloutsos, P: S. Yu, and T. Eliassi-Rad. Gateway finder in large graphs: problem definitions and fast solutions. *Inf. Retr.*, 15(3-4):391–411, 2012.
12. E. Zhong, W. Fan, and Q. Yang. User Behavior Learning and Transfer in Composite Social Networks. *ACM Trans. Knowl. Discov. D.*, 8(1):art. 6, 2014.

Chapter 8
Bringing Lurking in Game Theory

Abstract In this chapter, we describe the Lurker Game, i.e., a model for analyzing the transitions from a lurking to a non-lurking (i.e., active) user role, and vice versa, in terms of evolutionary game theory. A study carried out on different complex network models shows how the Lurker Game is suitable to model lurking dynamics, and how the adoption of rewarding mechanisms combined with the modeling of hypothetical heterogeneity of users' interests may lead users in an online community towards a cooperative behavior.

The attitude of users in OSNs continuously evolves over time. If we consider the analysis of the behavior of users as a system, from a network-wise point of view, this naturally calls for *game-theoretic* concepts to express the dynamics of users. Evolutionary games have indeed been successfully exploited to model OSNs dynamics [1, 7, 15, 19].

In the context of *user engagement dynamics* in OSNs (cf. Sect. 6.1), networked coordination games [6] enable the modeling of engagement property based on the notion of direct-benefit effects: users who want to gain an explicit benefit by remaining engaged should align their decision with one of their neighbors, so that the benefit increases as more neighbors decide to stay in the graph. In [14], the engagement property is considered in terms of a product-adoption process, and the engagement level of each user (i.e., her/his incentive to remain in the OSN) is determined proportionally to the associated core number, as computed by the k-core decomposition. Also, from the perspective of *social departure* [27] the skewness of the size distribution of the k-engagement subgraphs indicates that a large fraction of nodes does not have incentive to depart. However, it has been shown that users can depart independently of their engagement level, due to external factors. In other terms, real graphs tend in general to be vulnerable to targeted user departures, which might also be explained since most users in the OSN have low engagement. Social departure is also related to the problem of *churn prediction*, which is widely studied in the customer relationship management field (see [24] for a survey on this topic), and also applied to OSN contexts (e.g., [16]).

© The Author(s), under exclusive license to Springer Nature Switzerland AG 2018
A. Tagarelli, R. Interdonato, *Mining Lurkers in Online Social Networks*,
SpringerBriefs in Computer Science, https://doi.org/10.1007/978-3-030-00229-9_8

Within this view, the behavior of lurkers can suitably be modeled through *evolutionary game theory*. In this chapter, we will deepen this aspect by describing the **Lurker Game** proposed by the authors in [9], the first model for analyzing the transitions from a lurking to a non-lurking (i.e., active) user role, and vice versa, in terms of evolutionary game theory.

8.1 The Lurker Game

The game focuses on two macro-categories of users which correspond to the roles of active contributors and lurkers, and models a cooperator-defector game inspired by classic *public goods games* (PGGs) [17, 21, 22]. In PGGs, cooperators contribute to the system by adding some resource to a common pool, while defectors do not contribute. In **Lurker Game**, active users are regarded as contributors, while lurkers correspond to defectors.

In the **Lurker Game** model, information generated by contributors is expressed in terms of *virtual coin* (vc), which is assumed to be unitary by default. Given the OSN context, the term "information" is meant to include any type of social content produced in an OSN (i.e., posts, comments, preferences, etc.). The collective effort is represented by a *synergy factor r* ($r > 0$), which is usually adopted in PGGs and used to grant groups of cooperators.

While the above is modeled upon the classic PGG, **Lurker Game** shows two peculiarities related to OSN dynamics which differentiate it from the classic game. The first peculiarity is that, since the "public good" in **Lurker Game** is represented by the information generated by contributors, it is not divided but rather *equally shared* among all users of a group. The second peculiarity is that, in order to model topical interest of users, the authors introduce a further parameter, denoted by v, ranging in (0, 1], such that the common pool of virtual coins, shared in the OSN environment, is diversified by means of v. This helps in modeling heterogeneity of user interests and preferences, e.g., one may contribute by writing posts on a specific topic but it is not interested in reading about other topics.

8.1.1 Basic Dynamics

Given a set of N agents, the dynamics of **Lurker Game** unfolds in discrete time steps and it is defined as follows. At each time step, agents who take the role of cooperators have to put a virtual coin into the common pool, while the other agents (i.e., the ones taking the role of lurkers) do not take any action. The accumulated amount of virtual coins is increased by r and v, and then equally shared among all agents. The *payoff equations* in **Lurker Game** are defined as follows [9]:

$$\begin{cases} \pi^c = rv \sum_1^{N^c} vc - vc \\ \pi^d = rv \sum_1^{N^c} vc \end{cases} \qquad (8.1)$$

with N^c number of cooperators, r synergy factor, and v representing the heterogeneity of interests of users. Due to its evolutionary nature, **Lurker Game** allows agents to change their strategy [23], i.e., from cooperation to defection and vice versa. In particular, when considering two agents at a time, a Fermi-like function is adopted to implement a transition probability from one strategy to another. Given two agents x and y, this probability is defined as [9]:

$$W(s^x \rightarrow s^y) = \left(1 + \exp\left[\frac{\pi^y - \pi^x}{K}\right]\right)^{-1} \qquad (8.2)$$

where s^x and s^y denote the strategies of the players x and y, respectively, π^x and π^y denote their respective payoff, and K indicates uncertainty in adopting a strategy. By setting $K = 0.5$, a rational and meritocratic approach can be implemented during the strategy revision phase [21]. Like in the PGG, the Nash equilibrium of **Lurker Game** corresponds to defection, since behaving as defectors is much more convenient than behaving as cooperators.

8.1.2 Mean Field Analysis

The authors in [9] perform a *mean field* analysis [5] of **Lurker Game**, in order to investigate if the Nash equilibrium corresponds to the final ordered phase. Hence, it is assumed that the population is composed of only one big community and every agent interacts with all the others. Under this assumption, the evolution of a population with N agents is described by the following set of equations [11]:

$$\begin{cases} \frac{d\rho^c(t)}{dt} = p^c \cdot \rho^c(t) \cdot \rho^d(t) - p^d \cdot \rho^d(t) \cdot \rho^c(t) \\ \frac{d\rho^d(t)}{dt} = p^d \cdot \rho^d(t) \cdot \rho^c(t) - p^c \cdot \rho^c(t) \cdot \rho^d(t) \\ \rho^c(t) + \rho^d(t) = 1 \end{cases} \qquad (8.3)$$

with $\rho^c(t)$ and $\rho^d(t)$ densities of cooperators and defectors, $p^c(t)$ probability that cooperators prevail, and $p^d(t)$ probability that defectors prevail. These probabilities are computed according to the payoffs obtained, at each time step, by cooperators and defectors as defined in Eq. (8.1). Therefore, it should be considered the difference between the payoffs accumulated by the two agents randomly chosen at each time step. If we denote with x a cooperator and with y a defector, the probability p^c corresponds to $W(x \rightarrow y)$, so we consider the difference $\pi^d - \pi^c$, while, p^d corresponds to $W(y \rightarrow x)$, then we consider $\pi^c - \pi^d$. Few algebraic steps lead to the following solutions [9]:

$$\begin{cases} \pi^d - \pi^c = rvN\rho^c - rvN\rho^c + 1 = 1 \\ \pi^c - \pi^d = rvN\rho^c - 1 - rvN\rho^c = -1 \end{cases} \qquad (8.4)$$

By substituting results of Eq. (8.4) in Eq. (8.2), one obtains $p^c \sim 0.12$ and $p^d \sim 0.88$. Remarkably, the mean field approach to **Lurker Game** leads to dynamics completely independent both from r and v. Given the values computed in Eq. (8.4), the solution of the system in Eq. (8.3) confirms the expected result, i.e., defection prevails according to the Nash equilibrium.

8.1.3 Rewarding Mechanisms

The result of their mean field analysis leads the authors in [9] to focus on *rewarding mechanisms* in order to describe a model where population is driven towards an ordered phase of cooperation. When dealing with lurking behaviors, a rewarding mechanism can be seen as an integrated model for delurking: in fact, as previously discussed (cf. Chap. 6), the use of rewarding-based external stimuli is a frequently used type of delurking action—in this context, it is easy to figure out a practical application of rewarding mechanisms in *gamification* strategies [18] and *badge* assignments [2].

One important aspect is that contributors might be granted over time. Within this view, a key issue is how to decide the amount of rewards to engage lurkers, thus promoting the role of contributors. Intuitively, providing rewards too frequently would reduce the significance of the process, but if it is too difficult to get rewarded, one may give up and turn back again to lurking.

Therefore, a variation in the basic formulation of **Lurker Game** is proposed in [9] by introducing a *prize* structure for promoting cooperation. The payoff equation of cooperators is then modified as follows [9]:

$$\begin{cases} \pi^c = rv \sum_1^{N^c} vc - vc + \Phi(\Delta t^c) \\ \pi^d = rv \sum_1^{N^c} vc \end{cases} \qquad (8.5)$$

with $\Phi(\Delta t^c)$ *rewarding* function that allows cooperators to receive a further amount of virtual coins. This function takes in input Δt^c, i.e., the amount of time each agent behaves as a cooperator. The prize structure S grants cooperative agents at a fixed rate, i.e., every k time steps: $S : \Delta t^c = \{k, k, \ldots, k\}$. This way, each prize

---

Algorithm 1 Lurker Game [9]

Input: A population of N agents, where N^c are cooperators and N^d are defectors ($N = N^c + N^d$).
   The synergy factor $r > 0$.
   The user preference coefficient $v \in (0, 1]$.
   A network topology G that models the connectivity of the N agents, otherwise agents are fully
   connected to each other (mean field).
1: **repeat**
2:   Compute the payoff of cooperators and defectors, according to Eq. (8.5)
3:   Randomly select two agents x and y (with different strategies) s.t. x, y are linked w.r.t. G
4:   Agent y takes the strategy of agent x according to Eq. (8.2)
5: **until** all agents have the same behavior (Nash equilibrium)

---

consists of an amount of vc equal to that paid by a cooperator over time (between
two achieved prizes). The *prize function* is defined as follows [9]:

$$\Phi(\Delta t^c) = \begin{cases} \Delta t^c \cdot vc & \text{if } \Delta t^c \in S \\ 0 & \text{if } \Delta t^c \notin S \end{cases} \tag{8.6}$$

Analogously to the basic dynamics of **Lurker Game**, after every iteration agents
undergo a strategy revision phase based on Eq. (8.2). Algorithm 1 [9] sketches the
main steps performed in **Lurker Game**.

8.2   Lurker Game on Networks

In order to simulate its behavior in an OSN-like environment, the authors in [9]
carry out a study of the **Lurker Game** on complex networks. Following the lead
of previous studies on evolutionary games (e.g., [7, 12, 13, 15, 20, 25]), they focus
on two relevant models: Barabasi-Albert model [3] and Watts-Strogatz [26] model.
The well-known topological properties of these models (see, e.g., [4]) allow to easily
find relations between the outcomes of the analyzed model and the target network.

The Barabasi-Albert model generates scale-free networks, i.e., networks characterized by the presence of nodes with a very high degree, defined hubs. The
Watts-Strogatz model generates different kinds of networks by tuning a rewiring
parameter, β, which ranges within $[0, 1]$; in particular, $\beta = 0$ yields a regular ring
lattice topology, intermediate values of β yield small-world-networks (characterized
by relatively low average path lengths and high clustering coefficients), while
completely random networks are obtained for high values of β. In [9], the following
values are considered: $\beta = \{0.0, 0.3, 0.5, 0.8\}$. Figure 8.1 shows a pictorial
representation of each kind of network.

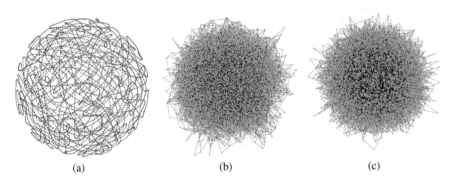

Fig. 8.1 Evaluation networks: (**a**) Watts-Strogatz with $\beta = 0.0$, (**b**) Watts-Strogatz with $\beta = 0.5$, (**c**) Barabasi-Albert [9]

Differently from the mean field case (which basically corresponds to a fully-connected network), when adopting complex networks only few agents are considered at each iteration. In particular, at each time step two randomly chosen agents play **Lurker Game** with all groups of belonging. Therefore, the accumulated payoffs are computed for each group and the final prize is assigned only to cooperative agents that played the game. Next, as previously discussed, the x-th agent tries to enforce its strategy to the y-th agent with probability defined in Eq. (8.2).

Memoryless and Memory-Aware Payoff.   When considering a complex network context, the authors in [9] introduce in the **Lurker Game** model an aspect related to the way agents manage their accumulated payoffs, by distinguishing between two scenarios of payoff accumulation, namely *memoryless* and *memory-aware*.

In the memoryless case, every time two agents are selected to play **Lurker Game** with their groups, they reset their accumulated payoff. Therefore, when computing the transition probability of Eq. (8.2), they consider only the payoff accumulated during the present time step. Instead, in the memory-aware case agents save their payoff over time. While memory-aware case is closer to a real scenario (e.g., online users typically accumulate rewards over time), the memoryless case avoids noise effects in numerical simulations that can emerge in Eq. (8.2) for large payoffs.

A *cutoff* is also introduced in the difference between the payoffs of the two considered agents (i.e., x and y). In doing so, for large payoffs, the Fermi function behaves like a simple rule with only two possible results: 1 and 0, i.e., 1 if the payoff of the x-th agent is greater than that of the y-th, and 0 otherwise. Thus, the granularity introduced by the Fermi function in terms of transition probabilities is lost, in the memory-aware case, after few time steps.

It is also relevant to observe that a similar problem may arise when dealing with scale-free networks since, even in the memoryless case, nodes with high degree (i.e., hubs) can accumulate at each iteration a very high payoff. As a result, the expected result is that simulations performed on scale-free networks in the memoryless case should yield outcomes similar to those achieved by the memory-aware case, at least by considering the same topology (i.e., scale-free in both cases).

Identifying Critical Parameters. The experimental analysis proposed in [9] exploits numerical simulations with the goal of identifying critical values of k and ν, i.e., the step adopted in the prize structure S and the variety of information (or users' interests) in the social network, respectively. These values, together with the final equilibrium achieved in both networks, provide a useful indicator for studying the dynamics of **Lurker Game** and for comparing different network topologies. Under this view, the **Lurker Game** deals with a disordered system [8, 10, 11], in terms of states (i.e., cooperators and defectors), having only two possible equilibria: either characterized by the prevalence of one of the species (i.e., cooperators or defectors) or characterized by a coexistence of both species at equilibrium. The former corresponds to a ferromagnetic phase, whereas the latter to a paramagnetic phase [10]. Thus, both the Nash equilibrium and its opposite case correspond to the ferromagnetic phase. The paramagnetic phase has been observed in games like the PGG, obtained by tuning the synergy factor and without adopting rewarding mechanisms [21].

Results of the experimental analysis carried out by the authors in [9] suggest that **Lurker Game** has a rich behavior, which can be described by considering the main degrees of freedom of the system: ν, k, network topology and the evolution of payoffs over time.

As regards Watts-Strogatz networks, in the memoryless case, for each considered β, a well recognized critical ν was found. In particular, by increasing β, cooperators require a smaller ν to prevail. This suggests that, in general, random topologies support cooperation better than regular ones. On the other hand, results achieved by memory-aware agents indicate that, in general, critical ν are smaller than those found in the memory-less case. However, the authors found that even for values greater than the minimal threshold of ν, sometimes defectors may prevail. The authors ascribe this phenomenon to the noise that may arise resulting from high payoffs

Concerning the simulations run on the Barabasi-Albert model, a major finding was that cooperators need a smaller ν to prevail than those computed in Watts-Strogatz network. Moreover, scale-free networks in the memory-aware case show an interesting bistable behavior for small values of ν. The authors suggest again that this may result from noise introduced by the utilization of large payoff in the Fermi function that they faced by adding a numerical cutoff. Conclusions drawn by the authors in [9] about scale-free networks are in accord with those reported in [17], since this type of networks have already been found to foster cooperation better than other topologies. Also, like for Watts-Strogatz networks, critical ν are robust to variations of k in the considered range.

Overall, the behavior of **Lurker Game** suggests that the adoption of rewarding mechanisms combined with the modeling of hypothetical heterogeneity of users' interests (ν) may lead a population towards cooperation. This supports the authors' initial intuition that **Lurker Game** can be used as a model to explain lurking-delurking transitions dynamics.

References

1. G. Abramson and M. Kuperman. Social games in social networks. *Physical Review E*, 63, 2001.
2. A. Anderson, D. Huttenlocher, J. Kleinberg, and J. Leskovec. Steering user behavior with badges. In *Proc. ACM Conf. on World Wide Web (WWW)*, 2013.
3. A.L. Barabasi and R. Albert. Emergence of scaling in random networks. *Science*, 286:509–512, 1999.
4. A.L. Barabasi and R. Albert. Statistical mechanics of complex networks. *Reviews of Modern Physics*, 74:47–97, 2002.
5. A. Barra. The mean field Ising model trough interpolating techniques. *Journal of Statistical Physics*, 132-5:787–809, 2008.
6. D. Easley and J. Kleinberg. *Networks, Crowds, and Markets: Reasoning about a highly connected world*. Cambridge University Press, 2010.
7. F. Fu, D.I. Rosenbloom, L. Wang, and M.A. Nowak. Imitation dynamics of vaccination behavior on social networks. *The Royal Society - Proc. B*, 278, 2011.
8. S. Galam and B. Walliser. Ising model versus normal form game. *Physica A*, 389:481–489, 2010.
9. M. A. Javarone, R. Interdonato, and A. Tagarelli. *Complex Networks VII: Proc. of the 7th Workshop on Complex Networks CompleNet 2016*, chapter Modeling Evolutionary Dynamics of Lurking in Social Networks, pages 227–239. 2016.
10. M.A. Javarone. Is poker a skill game? new insights from statistical physics. *EPL*, 110, 2015.
11. M.A. Javarone. Statistical physics of the spatial prisoner's dilemma with memory-aware agents. *arxiv:1509.04558*, 2015.
12. M.A. Javarone and A.E. Atzeni. The role of competitiveness in the prisoner's dilemma. *Computational Social Networks*, 2, 2015.
13. E. Lieberman, C. Hauert, and M.A. Nowak. Evolutionary dynamics on graphs. *Nature*, 433:312–316, 2004.
14. F. D. Malliaros and M. Vazirgiannis. To stay or not to stay: modeling engagement dynamics in social graphs. In *Proc. ACM Conf. on Information and Knowledge Management (CIKM)*, pages 469–478, 2013.
15. M. Perc, J. Gomez-Gardenes, A. Szolnoki, L.M. Floria, and Y. Moreno. Evolutionary dynamics of group interactions on structured populations: a review. *J. R. Soc. Interface*, 10-80, 2013.
16. M. Rowe. Mining user lifecycles from online community platforms and their application to churn prediction. In *Proc. IEEE Int. Conf. on Data Mining (ICDM)*, pages 637–646, 2013.
17. F. C. Santos, M. D. Santos, and J. M. Pacheco. Social diversity promotes the emergence of cooperation in public goods games. *Nature*, 454:231–216, 2008.
18. K. Seaborn and D.I. Fels. Gamification in theory and action: A survey. *International Journal of Human-Computer Studies*, 74:14–31, 2015.
19. S. Van Segbroeck, F. C. Santos, T. Lenaerts, and J.M. Pacheco. Reacting differently to adverse ties promotes cooperation in social networks. *Physical Review Letters*, 102(058105), 2009.
20. G. Szabo and G. Fath. Evolutionary games on graphs. *Physics Reports*, 446, 2007.
21. A. Szolnoki and M. Perc. Reward and cooperation in the spatial public goods game. *EPL*, 92, 2010.
22. A. Szolnoki, G. Szabo, and M. Perc. Phase diagrams for the spatial public goods game with pool punishment. *Physical Review E*, 83, 2011.
23. M. Tomassini. Introduction to evolutionary game theory. 2014.
24. T. Vafeiadis, K. I. Diamantaras, G. Sarigiannidis, and K. Ch. Chatzisavvas. A comparison of machine learning techniques for customer churn prediction. *Simulation Modelling Practice and Theory*, 55:1–9, 2015.

25. Z. Wang, A. Szolnoki, and M. Perc. Interdependent network reciprocity in evolutionary games. *Scientific Reports*, 3-1183, 2013.
26. D.J. Watts and S.H. Strogatz. Collective dynamics of small-world networks. *Nature*, 393:440–442, 1998.
27. S. Wu, A. D. Sarma, A. Fabrikant, S. Lattanzi, and A. Tomkins. Arrival and departure dynamics in social networks. In *Proc. ACM Conf. on Web Search and Web Data Mining (WSDM)*, pages 233–242, 2013.

Chapter 9
Concluding Remarks and Challenges

Abstract This chapter ends the brief offering a summary of the main topics discussed and providing suggestions for future research.

Lurking behaviors have been long studied in social science and human-computer interaction fields. Over the last few years, this study has also matured in social network analysis and mining, and in related fields in computer science and complex network systems. In this view, we have taken the opportunity of offering a survey on research on lurking behavior analysis in online social networks, with an emphasis on recent developments from a network science and data mining perspectives. Figure 9.1 provides a conceptual map that concisely illustrates the state-of-the-art of models developed, major computational problems addressed, and the types of data and social networks relatively examined so far in the literature and discussed in this brief.

We have emphasized the essential role of centrality and ranking methods as key-enabling factor to identify lurkers and analyze their behaviors. We have highlighted the pervasiveness of the notion of lurking and its differently shaped manifestations, from social media platforms to collaboration networks and trust networks. We have provided evidence of both theoretical and practical significance of existing lurker ranking methods over different social network ecosystems. Network analysis paradigms and techniques (e.g., preferential attachment, reciprocity and responsiveness analysis, percolation analysis) as well as data mining tools (e.g., time series clustering, topic modeling) have been largely utilized to address a plethora of computational problems related to lurking behaviors. We have raised the emergence for developing computational approaches to delurk users that take a silent role in the community life, and in this regard, targeted influence maximization methods have been proposed as an appealing solution. Moreover, integrating notions of community-oriented and diversity-aware influence maximization into a delurking task has revealed to further enhance opportunities for the engagement of lurkers. Yet according to boundary spanning, and projecting it to the interrelation between multiple OSN platforms, we have analyzed how members who lurk inside an OSN may not lurk, or even take on the role of contributors/experts in other OSNs. Finally,

© The Author(s), under exclusive license to Springer Nature Switzerland AG 2018   87
A. Tagarelli, R. Interdonato, *Mining Lurkers in Online Social Networks*,
SpringerBriefs in Computer Science, https://doi.org/10.1007/978-3-030-00229-9_9

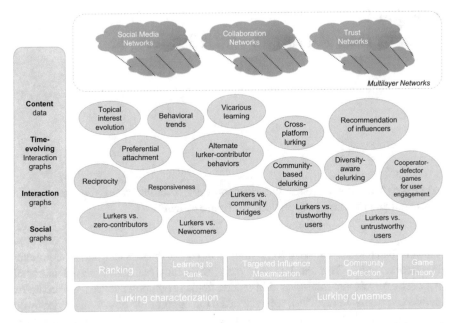

Fig. 9.1 Computational approaches to lurking behavior analysis and mining: state-of-the-art of methods, algorithms, problems, data types and source environments

we have discussed how lurking and delurking dynamics can intuitively be modeled and analyzed through evolutionary game theory.

Through this survey, we aimed to pursue a twofold goal. The first goal is to increase the visibility of lurking behavior analysis and mining as a valuable research topic, and to favor the bridging of different disciplines that are closely related with respect to this topic. Within this view, we hope that the survey lurking behavior analysis and mining offered in this brief can be of support to scholars and practitioners that are involved in different research fields. The second goal is to pave the way for next-generation models and techniques that can cope with a large, previously unexplored set of related problems and applications in social networks. We are indeed aware that still many problems remain open and many opportunities are worth to be considered.

9.1   Modeling Lurking Behaviors Through Latent Interactions

One important aspect is that existing lurker mining methods are designed to discover lurking behaviors by mainly focusing on models built on user relationships that correspond to a social graph or an interaction graph, both in static and dynamic network scenarios (and of course, in case, topic-biased contexts). In other terms, we have seen that existing lurker mining methods are fed with *visible, publicly traceable* information-production and information-consumption activities performed by users, upon the assumption that any two users are related to each other at least via a followship relation. Nevertheless, one might certainly argue that a (publicly traceable) followship is not a necessary condition for a user to be interested in others' contents and activities, thus in the community life: what really matters should also refer to the *latent* or *silent* interactions of users, i.e., non-publicly-traceable browsing, reading, or watching activities in the OSN environment. Unfortunately, it is not easy to build OSN datasets that are resource-rich in terms of latent interactions, mainly due to privacy policies and API limitations currently imposed by all main OSN services. But, as hard as it is to challenge, learning lurker mining methods through latent information-consumption activities represents a big opportunity to enhance our understanding of lurking behaviors. Within this view, valuable suggestions can be drawn from the (relatively little) work concerning latent activities of OSN users, such as [17] on RenRen users' profile visits, [3] on traffic and session patterns of user workloads (based on clickstream data collected through a Brazilian OSN-aggregator website), and [4, 5] on a comparison of Facebook users' visible and hidden actions.

Moreover, by exploiting hidden activities of users and latent user interactions, better delurking strategies could be developed. In particular, within a targeted influence maximization approach like that proposed in [6, 16], we believe that the stage of learning of influence probabilities for the diffusion graph model would greatly benefit from richer information about users' behaviors. Also, in this context, exploiting information on latent user interactions can be crucial to characterize the effect of hidden network structures on information diffusion processes [2].

9.2 Emotion-Driven Analysis of Lurkers

Emotions have been largely studied and theorized, resulting in several models for interpreting and characterizing emotions [24]. One exemplary model is the well-known Plutchik's wheel of emotions [25] which, based on eight primary emotions (i.e., joy, sadness, anger, fear, trust, disgust, surprise, anticipation), allows for explaining different degrees of intensity and corresponding bipolarities using a graphical circumplex model.

A further appealing direction in our opinion for pushing towards research on lurker analysis and mining comes from the opportunity of handling a great deal of knowledge represented by how users express *emotions* while interacting with others, or simply while consuming information. In this regard, advanced computational learning approaches that would be of great benefit include, e.g., deep learning for the construction of computational models of emotion [22], sentiment data flow analysis [26], and other developments in natural language processing [7].

9.3 Psycho-Sociological Influences on Lurkers

The psycho-sociological background of an individual plays a crucial role in determining her/his status and dynamics within an (online) social environment. For instance, psycho-sociological factors are important to shape the individual's inclination and attitude towards certain moods or feelings that s/he may have when approaching to specific social events, or the role that s/he may take in response to them. In this respect, several psychological theories and models exist that can explain and help model the multifaceted nature of psycho-sociological influencing factors. For instance, besides the aforementioned Plutchik's wheel of emotions, other conceptual models have been conceived as tools for supporting the classification and analysis of psychological and sociological factors outside the sphere of the emotions. One example is the Big5 *personality* model [14], which focuses on the personality dimensions of openness, conscientiousness, extroversion, agreeableness, and neuroticism; another example is the Schwartz Values model [27], which considers the following *value* types: achievement, benevolence, conformity, hedonism, security, self-direction, stimulation, tradition, and universalism. More-over, the individual's attitude and stance towards an event can be explained in terms of a number of theories. For instance, *affective forecasting* [30] explains how individuals are biased when reacting to social events in which they are involved; related to this are the so-called *endowment effect* [18] and *negativity bias* [19], where the former indicates the positive or overestimation effect of the ownership on the individual's interpretation of events, and the latter suggests that negative things or facts (e.g., unpleasant thoughts, negative social interactions, traumatic events) have a greater effect on one's psychological state than neutral or positive things or facts.

We believe that all of such theories and models can represent valuable resources to develop advanced computational approaches for social network analysis and mining. Particularly, psycho-sociological theories and models become essential to cope with critical and sociologically unbearable situations that nowadays, more and more often, affect individuals of any age or gender and their OSN life. In this context, we argue that many psychologically critical situations occurring in an OSN directly involve lurkers. Two notable of such situations are discussed next.

- **Lurkers vs. Bystanders: The Cyberbullying Case.** *Cyberbullying* refers to any intentional, often reiterated, verbal act of aggression or harassment carried out by an individual or group against others, and mediated through some form of electronic contact. Over the last decade and as a result of the increased availability of new technologies, cyberbullying has become a serious issue in many OSN platforms. Research studies from different disciplines have attempted to define the main causes and provide regulatory frameworks to prevent and combat cyberbullying. In doing this, most of the early studies have traditionally focused on two types of roles, the victim and the bully. On the other hand, research consistently shows that intervening to stop the bullying activity and/or offering help to a victim is more rare than not. This is explained by the *bystander effect*, or bystander apathy, which is a group behavioral pattern first studied in socio-psychology [9] whereby an individual is less likely to take action to provide help to a victim when other people are present in an emergency situation, because s/he believes that other bystanders will eventually step in and act in some way. Whenever a bystander would decide to take part to the emergency and be actively involved in the event, this will significantly change the balance either in favor of the victim or the bully (the latter is likely to happen if the bystander is a friend of the bully) [1].

With cyberbullying on the rise in many OSN contexts, there has been an increased attention in research on bystander intervention from a social science and human-computer interaction perspective (e.g., [10, 29]). Nevertheless, it would also be important to define computational methods that can aid to perform bystander intervention on OSNs. Within this view, we argue that, as chance spectator, a bystander stands in analogy with a lurker who witnesses an emergency through social media. Therefore, we speculate that user engagement and delurking tools can provide a valuable support in terms of bystander intervention as well.

- **Lurkers and Health: The Depression and Suicide Prevention in OSNs.** Another social concern refers to the increase in psychological depression states that often involve OSN users. A consequent challenge is to develop new technologies for the early identification of individuals with behavioral traits that can be related to psychological depression states, or even to suicide commitments, and that can be recognized as "at-risk" through their use of the OSNs. Depression and suicide commitment reflect some serious personal issue but often are linked to a deterioration of the (online) social context in which an individual lives. Risk factors are multiple and complex, including changes in personal relationships, addiction, unemployment, and also harassment and (cyber)bullying [23].

Again in this context, we believe that lurking behavior analysis methods can aid to better understand inclination to depression and suicide commitment, and to eventually prevent episodes by persuading some of the users that are reticent to interact with others to change their status and to have more favorable outlooks of their life.

9.4 Dis/Misinformation, Fake News, and Lurkers

Besides their original social purpose, OSNs have gained a central role as the preferred mean not only to share and discuss news, but also to actively shape public opinion. Nevertheless, the structure of social platforms has shown different drawbacks that make it easy to devise, in addition to legitimate communication strategies, disinformation campaigns that leverage on the viral dissemination of *fake news* [21]. The so-called "echo chamber" phenomenon [12, 13] (i.e., a context where beliefs are reinforced due to their diffusion in tight homophily-based communities) tends to quickly transform *disinformation* [20] (i.e., voluntary dissemination of fake news) into *misinformation* [8, 15, 28] (i.e., dissemination of a fake news that is believed to be true). Recently, dis/misinformation campaigns have been proven to be able to influence the outcome of events of crucial importance (e.g., political elections [11]). While it is often possible to debunk fake news once they gained global popularity, it is challenging to trace them back to the original source, or stop their diffusion while they are still circulating in a limited-closed community context. Since disseminating fake news can be recognized as a crime (or, at least, as an "unethical" behavior), the profiles used to perform these actions typically do not refer to influential users in the networks—who could easily be traced back or recognized as untrustworthy once they have been part of previous campaigns—but rather to profiles with low activity rates (often created ad-hoc for this purpose), which join communities as peripheral nodes just to trigger the viral circulation of the news.

In this regard, we can recognize a clear parallel between lurkers and profiles used to start dis/misinformation campaigns. We argue that the methods used to identify and analyze lurkers can profitably be adapted to recognize profiles inside online communities which can be potentially used to start misinformation campaigns, thus supporting prevention and containment tasks.

References

1. Sara Bastiaensens, Heidi Vandebosch, Karolien Poels, Katrien Van Cleemput, Ann DeSmet, and Ilse De Bourdeaudhuij. Cyberbullying on social network sites. An experimental study into bystanders' behavioural intentions to help the victim or reinforce the bully. *Computers in Human Behavior*, 31:259–271, 2014.
2. V. Belák, A. J. Mashhadi, A. Sala, and D. Morrison. Phantom cascades: The effect of hidden nodes on information diffusion. *Computer Communications*, 73:12–21, 2016.
3. F. Benevenuto, T. Rodrigues, M. Cha, and V. Almeida. Characterizing user navigation and interactions in online social networks. *Information Sciences*, 195:1–24, 2012.
4. M. S. Bernstein, E. Bakshy, M. Burke, and B. Karrer. Quantifying the invisible audience in social networks. In *Proc. ACM Conf. on Human Factors in Computing Systems (CHI)*, pages 21–30, 2013.
5. M. Burke, C. Marlow, and T. Lento. Social network activity and social well-being. In *Proc. ACM Conf. on Human Factors in Computing Systems (CHI)*, pages 1909–1912, 2010.
6. A. Caliò, R. Interdonato, C. Pulice, and A. Tagarelli. Topology-driven diversity for targeted influence maximization with application to user engagement in social networks. *IEEE Transactions on Knowledge and Data Engineering*, 2018.
7. E. Cambria and B. White. Jumping NLP curves: A review of natural language processing research. *IEEE Computational Intelligence Magazine*, 9(2):48–57, 2014.
8. Giovanni Luca Ciampaglia, Alexios Mantzarlis, Gregory Maus, and Filippo Menczer. Research challenges of digital misinformation: Toward a trustworthy web. *AI Magazine*, 39(1):65–74, 2018.
9. J. M. Darley and B. Latané. Bystander intervention in emergencies: Diffusion of responsibility. *Journal of Personality and Social Psychology*, 8(4):377–383, 1968.
10. Dominic DiFranzo, Samuel Hardman Taylor, Franccesca Kazerooni, Olivia D. Wherry, and Natalya N. Bazarova. Upstanding by design: Bystander intervention in cyberbullying. In *Proc. ACM Conf. on Human Factors in Computing Systems (CHI)*, page 211, 2018.

11. Emilio Ferrara. Disinformation and social bot operations in the run up to the 2017 french presidential election. *First Monday*, 22(8), 2017.

12. Kiran Garimella, Gianmarco De Francisci Morales, Aristides Gionis, and Michael Mathioudakis. Political discourse on social media: Echo chambers, gatekeepers, and the price of bipartisanship. In *Proceedings of the 2018 World Wide Web Conference on World Wide Web, WWW 2018, Lyon, France, April 23-27, 2018*, pages 913–922, 2018.

13. Nabeel Gillani, Ann Yuan, Martin Saveski, Soroush Vosoughi, and Deb Roy. Me, my echo chamber, and I: introspection on social media polarization. In *Proceedings of the 2018 World Wide Web Conference on World Wide Web, WWW 2018, Lyon, France, April 23-27, 2018*, pages 823–831, 2018.

14. L. R. Goldberg. The structure of phenotypic personality traits. *American Psychologist*, 48(1):26, 1993.

15. Pik-Mai Hui, Chengcheng Shao, Alessandro Flammini, Filippo Menczer, and Giovanni Luca Ciampaglia. The Hoaxy misinformation and fact-checking diffusion network. In *Proc. Int. Conf. on Weblogs and Social Media (ICWSM)*, pages 528–530, 2018.

16. R. Interdonato, C. Pulice, and A. Tagarelli. "Got to have faith!": The DEvOTION algorithm for delurking in social networks. In *Proc. Int. Conf. on Advances in Social Networks Analysis and Mining (ASONAM)*, pages 314–319, 2015.

17. J. Jiang, C. Wilson, X. Wang, W. Sha, P. Huang, Y. Dai, and B. Y. Zhao. Understanding latent interactions in online social networks. *ACM Trans. on the Web*, 7(4):18, 2013.

18. E. J. Johnson, G. Hubl, and A. Keinan. Aspects of endowment: a query theory of value construction. *Journal of Experimental Psychology Learning Memory Cognition*, 33(3):461, 2007.

19. D. E. Kanouse and L. R. Hanson Jr. Negativity in evaluations. In *Attribution: Perceiving the causes of behavior*. Hillsdale, NJ, US: Lawrence Erlbaum Associates, Inc., 1987.

20. Srijan Kumar, Robert West, and Jure Leskovec. Disinformation on the web: Impact, characteristics, and detection of Wikipedia hoaxes. In *Proc. ACM Conf. on World Wide Web (WWW)*, pages 591–602, 2016.

21. Volodymyr Lysenko and Catherine Brooks. Russian information troops, disinformation, and democracy. *First Monday*, 23(5), 2018.

22. H. P. Martínez, Y. Bengio, and G. N. Yannakakis. Learning Deep Physiological Models of Affect. *IEEE Computational Intelligence Magazine*, 8(2):20–33, 2013.

23. World Health Organization. *Preventing suicide: A global imperative*. Geneva, Switzerland: World Health Organization, 2014.

24. A. Ortony and T. J. Turner. What's basic about basic emotions? *Psychological Review*, 97:315–331, 1990.

25. Robert Plutchik and Henry Kellerman. *Emotion: Theory, research, and experience: Vol. 1. Theories of emotion*. Elsevier Inc., 1980.

26. S. Poria, E. Cambria, A. F. Gelbukh, F. Bisio, and A. Hussain. Sentiment Data Flow Analysis by Means of Dynamic Linguistic Patterns. *IEEE Computational Intelligence Magazine*, 10(4):26–36, 2015.

27. Shalom H. Schwartz. Universals in the Content and Structure of Values: Theoretical Advances and Empirical Tests in 20 Countries. *Advances in Experimental Social Psychology*, 25:1–65, 1992.

28. Jieun Shin, Lian Jian, Kevin Driscoll, and François Bar. The diffusion of misinformation on social media: Temporal pattern, message, and source. *Computers in Human Behavior*, 83:278–287, 2018.

29. Jiyeon Song and Insoo Oh. Factors influencing bystanders' behavioral reactions in cyberbullying situations. *Computers in Human Behavior*, 78:273–282, 2018.

30. T. D. Wilson and D. T. Gilbert. Affective forecasting: Knowing what to want. *Current Directions in Psychological Science*, 14(3):131–134, 2010.

Printed in the United States
By Bookmasters